THE STORY

OF THE

STEWARTS

AFTER BANNOCKBURN.

WALTER, STEWART OF SCOTLAND, RECEIVING THE
PRINCESS MARJORY BRUS AND HER COMPANIONS
IN CAPTIVITY. [*page* 75

Facsimile Reprint

Published 1993 by

HERITAGE BOOKS, INC.
1540-E Pointer Ridge Place, Bowie, MD 20716
(301) 390-7709

ISBN 1-55613-866-0

A Complete Catalog Listing Hundreds of Titles
on History, Genealogy, and Americana Available
Free upon Request

The Story of the Stewarts

. . . SECRETO . WALTERI . FIL . ALA . .

(Private Seal of Walter the son of Alan.)

Printed for The Stewart Society

———

EDINBURGH:
GEORGE STEWART & CO.
1901

To Colonel the Honourable

WALTER STEWART,

in whom are mirrored the noble qualities of his
illustrious ancestors and kindred,

THIS STORY OF THEIR LIVES

is respectfully dedicated.

PREFACE.

The Story of the Stewarts related in the following pages, is the outcome of a lifelong indulgence in what to many will no doubt seem a great weakness and, perchance, to some a greater folly—the pride of name and race.

The notes from which it has been compiled were originally made solely for the writer's own use, but the institution of "The Stewart Society" has suggested the thought that to others, with possibly less time and opportunity, the information gathered might be no less interesting, and perhaps afford equal pleasure.

No pretence is made either to literary merit or original research. The facts collected from time to time, while perusing the works of various writers—ancient and modern—have simply been arranged in chronological or genealogical sequence so as to present some appearance of continuity. A list of the works which form the authority for the narrative is appended for the satisfaction of those curious in such details, but it has been thought that in this busy age the majority of readers will prefer to have their information presented to them in a concrete and already digested form, and that therefore the simple story will prove more attractive than one encumbered with a mass of references. The writer does not venture to hope that the book is entirely free from error, but certainly such mistakes as may have occurred are the result of accident or imperfect information—not of design.

Burns' patriotic dream or ambition was, that he
" For puir auld Scotland's sake
" Some usefu' plan or book could make
" Or sing a sang at least,"
and in a somewhat similar, if less lofty or comprehensive spirit, these pages are offered to the Members of The Stewart Society.

Not that we may, in contemplation of the former glories of our race, be induced to fold our hands in complacent self-esteem, content to rest on the laurels of our ancestors, but that from their life-history we may learn, while avoiding their weaknesses, to be, like them, strong in patriotism and self-sacrifice, in courage and fortitude, in loyalty to our friends, and in generosity to our enemies.

And, above and beyond all, that, as we have inherited a name ennobled by the deeds and the virtues of generations of warriors and patriots, we may see to it that in our hands, their name, and through it their honour, takes no stain.

AUTHORITIES FOR THE STORY.

Fordun's "Scotichronicon."

"Chronicle of Pluscarden."

Symson's "History of the Stewarts."

Duncan Stewart's "History of the Stewarts" (1739).

Lord Hailes's "Annals of Scotland."

Andrew Stuart's "History of the Stewarts."

Chalmers's "Caledonia."

Pinkerton's "History of Scotland."

Riddell's "Scottish Peerage Law."

Riddell's "Tracts, Legal and Historical."

Dunbar's "Kings of Scotland."

Agnew's "Hereditary Sheriffs of Galloway."

The Exchequer Rolls of Scotland.

"The Red Book of Menteith."

Napier's "Lennox of Auld."

"The Norman People."

Round's "Peerage and Family History."

Calendar of Documents preserved in France.

Reports of the Historical MS. Commission.

Etc.   Etc.

THE STORY OF THE STEWARTS.

O F the origin of this race, destined to give so many warriors, statesmen, and Kings to Scotland, and whose descendants are yet to be traced not only in the noblest families in this country and on the Continent, but in practically every reigning house in Europe, various accounts have been given, and over it much disputation has taken place.

For all practical purposes however, these accounts may be resolved into two, the old and the new—the former assigning to the Stewarts a native Scottish origin, and the latter a Norman or Breton one. The rival theories and arguments will be stated as shortly and concisely as possible, and the individual reader be left to form his own conclusion.

The ancient traditions of Scotland and all the older Scots historians confer on this family a purely native or Scottish origin, tracing their descent from Banquo, Shakespeare's "Thane of Lochaber," and through him from the ancient Kings of Scotland.

According to these accounts, Banquo, Thane of Lochaber, was the son of Ferquhard, Thane of Lochaber, who, again, was the son of Kenneth III., King of Scots. Banquo flourished in the reign of King Duncan, and along with his sovereign was murdered by Macbeth in 1043, leaving an only son, Fleance, who, to escape a like fate, fled to the Court of Llewellin ap Griffith, Prince of Wales, only, however, to meet at other hands the doom he had sought to shun at home. He is said to have fallen a victim within a few years of his arrival (1045 or 1047) to the jealousy of some of the Welsh lords whose ill-will he had incurred by his success in the favours of the Princess Nesta, the daughter of the Welsh Prince.

Walter, the son of Fleance by this lady, spent his youth at his grandfather's Court, but, as he grew up, the animosity which had taken the father's life extended to the son, and Walter in his turn had also to seek safety in a foreign land. Travelling first to the Court of Edward the Confessor, and next to that of Alan "the Red," Earl of Brittany, he ultimately attached himself to that Prince, to whom his mother Nesta is said to have been distantly related. There, following the example of his father, he won the favour of his protector's daughter, whom he married, and by whom he had a son, Alan. Walter thereafter accompanied his father-in-law, the Earl of Brittany, to the invasion of England, but having for some reason incurred the displeasure of the Conqueror, he retired into Scotland, where he was received with favour by King Malcolm, who made him his steward or cup-bearer. Walter is said to have died in 1093, and to have been succeeded by his son Alan, who, according to the same traditions, accompanied Godfrey de Bouillon to the Holy War, and was present at the capture of Jerusalem in 1099. Returning to Scotland in the reign of King Edgar, he was made Lord High Stewart, and dying in 1153, was succeeded by his son Walter, the first ancestor of the Stewarts who passes out of the region of tradition or hypothesis into the realm of sober and authentic history.

Such, stated succinctly, is the origin and pedigree assigned to the House of Stewart by the traditions and early historians of Scotland, and generally believed and accepted as correct for centuries.

It is noteworthy that the belief in these traditions was not confined to Scotland, but seems to have been shared by some English writers, while the story itself was at least utilised, if not actually accepted, by Shakespeare, who, in his " Macbeth," makes the witches prophesy to Banquo, " Thou shalt get kings tho' thou be none," and, in a later Act, conjure up before Macbeth a vision of kings of Banquo's line " that two-fold balls and treble sceptres carry "—prophetic of the sway of the Stewarts over these islands.

Mr George Burnet, the late Lyon King-of-Arms, considered it probable that the origin of these traditions might be traced to Barbour, the writer of the versified history of " The Bruce," who is known to have written another great poem on the Stewarts, in which he traced their ancestry through Banquo to the ancient Kings of Scotland; and even, working up the old fabled connection between the Scots and the Trojans, to Brutus, Prince of Troy. This epic has long been lost, but Wynton in his rhyming chronicle states that in it—

> " The Stewartis orygenalle
> " The Archdekyne has tretyd hale
> " In metyre fayre."

It is significant however, that Bower, the continuator of Fordun, another nearly contemporaneous writer, accuses Barbour of having misrepresented the origin of the Stewarts in his book "in the vulgar tongue."

At the time when these books were written, the real origin of the race, whether native or alien, must have been perfectly well known; and such a conflict of statement even in that age, renders the true position all the more uncertain to-day. Mr Burnet indeed suggests that Barbour was too much of a courtier to ascribe to his sovereign an English, or at least a foreign, ancestry; but on the other hand it seems incredible that even a courtier would have ventured, with no shadow of foundation whatever, to ascribe to the reigning family an origin which not only they but their subjects must in that case have perfectly well known to be baseless, and which could only expose both the writer and his heroes to ridicule.

As has been indicated, these traditionary accounts were implicitly accepted and believed in for centuries, but more recent research has caused them to be viewed with scepticism and at length, in many cases, with entire disbelief.

Lord Hailes, in his "Annals of Scotland," proved that some at least of these old legendary tales were unworthy of credit, and this view was shared by Andrew Stuart of Torrance in his "History of the Stuarts of Castlemilk" written last century. Neither was able, however, to give any information as to the real ancestry. Pinkerton, in his "History of Scotland," was the first to point to the probability of a connection with the great English family of Fitz-Alan, but it was reserved for Chalmers, the learned author of that great mine of information on Scottish antiquities — " Caledonia " — to produce new facts from which he constructed a pedigree for the Stewarts, of an entirely different character. It is unfortunate that Chalmers, though unquestionably a man of the deepest antiquarian lore and research, so frequently lays himself open to a suspicion of being governed by a desire to hold up to admiration the greater extent and depth of his own research as compared with the work of his predecessors, and even of overturning as many previously accepted ideas as possible, but his genealogical account of the Stewarts, while it completely upsets all the old traditions of the race, is yet so important and so circumstantial as to have carried conviction to the minds of most of those who have studied the two rival theories.

Chalmers then, arguing from the known to the unknown, begins with the life of the first authentic ancestor of the Stewarts—Walter, High Stewart of Scotland in the time of David I. and Malcolm IV. The outstanding event, so far as preserved, in his career was the foundation of Paisley Abbey in 1164, and the Foundation Charter of the Abbey is the source from which Chalmers draws the facts out of which he constructs the principal links in the chain of

B

his reasoning. In this Charter, Walter, Stewart of Scotland, describes himself as "Walterus filius Alani," and the same document discloses the fact that the monks who were to carry on the religious work of the Abbey were brought by Walter from a Cluniac monastery in Shropshire. At the time in question (1164) Wenlock, in Shropshire, was a great seat of this particular monastic order, while the principal baron of that neighbourhood was William Fitz-Alan, Lord of Oswestrie and Clune Castle. This William was, as his name indicates, the son of Alan, who in his turn is proved to have been Lord of Oswestrie and Sheriff of Shropshire after the Norman Conquest. Alan, Lord of Oswestrie, in addition to this his eldest son, William, had another son, Walter, as is proved by the English "Liber nigeria Scaccarii," in which, about the year 1154, "Walter, the son of Alan," appears as vassal holding lands of the value of two knights' fee under "William, the son of Alan, of Salopscire"; while further proof is found in a charter of 1185, in which "William, the son of Alan," granted to the Order of Knights Templars the towns of Carditon, Huchemerse, etc., and "Walter, the son of Alan," granted them part of Coveton.

From these facts—

(1) The designation of "Walter, the son of Alan," in the Foundation Charter of Paisley Abbey and in the grant of lands in Shropshire to the Hospital of St John (Knights Templars);

(2) the importation of Cluniac monks from Shropshire to carry on the work of Paisley Abbey; and

(3) the existence of an "Alan," Sheriff of Shropshire, and father of two sons, William and Walter—

Chalmers argues that in the said "Alan" and "William" we have the father and elder brother of Walter, High Stewart of Scotland under David I. and Malcolm IV., Kings of Scots. The elder of those two brothers unquestionably became the ancestor of the Earls of Arundel in England, and the younger is held by Chalmers and his followers to have been the ancestor of the House of Stewart.

As regards the events or circumstances which led Walter to transfer his allegiance to Scotland, Chalmers relates that William Fitz-Alan, Lord of Oswestrie, was a close friend of the Earl of Gloucester, natural son of Henry I. of England, the chief supporter of that monarch's daughter, Matilda, against the attempts of her nephew, Stephen of Boulogne, to snatch from her the English crown. Matilda's rights to her father's throne were also stoutly asserted by her uncle, David I., King of Scots, who invaded England, and was there joined by Gloucester and Fitz-Alan with their retainers. Chalmers suggests that the Lord of Oswestrie on that occasion was not improbably accompanied by his younger brother Walter, and that Walter at this time attached himself to the Scottish king.

There is certainly nothing inherently improbable in this theoretical pedigree, and it moreover derives some confirmation from a later event, which, however wild and unreasonable it may in itself appear according to modern ideas, is not without interest in the present connection.

During the wars which followed Bruce's death, and the minority of David II., the young Stewart of Scotland—the lineal descendant of this Walter, and subsequently known in history as Robert II., King of Scots—was a fugitive, outlawed for his patriotism by the usurper Baliol, his lands given to a Scoto-English baron, and his titles forfeited. In these circumstances it pleased the English to regard him as non-existent, and his office of High Stewart of Scotland was thereupon claimed by Richard Fitz-Alan, Earl of Arundel,—one of the commanders of Edward III.'s army,—as his by hereditary right. Not only so, but the Tower Records show that Edward III. was so desirous of himself acquiring the office of Stewart of Scotland that he purchased Arundel's shadowy rights, and subsequently obtained from the compliant Baliol a confirmation of the office in his own person.

This claim by the Earl of Arundel, in conjunction with the other coincident circumstances mentioned, seems to place it almost beyond question that Chalmers' theory is correct, and that "Walter the son of Alan," who received the office of Great Steward of Scotland from David I., was in truth the younger brother of William Fitz-Alan, the direct ancestor of the Earl in question.

Alan, the father of William Fitz-Alan (and who, from the records quoted, also clearly had another son called Walter), appears in English history as early as 1101, in which year he witnessed a Charter by Henry I. to the Bishop of Norwich, and another by the Bishop himself relative to the formation of a Cathedral Priory. The latter document is of further interest, however, as in it the Bishop confirms a grant previously made by Alan himself to the Priory, of the church and tithes of Langham in Norfolk, thereby proving that Alan must have been settled, and possessed lands in Norfolk, prior to 1101.

In 1102 he was appointed Sheriff of Shropshire by Henry I., and from the same king he also received the Manor of Eaton, which, with Henry's sanction, he afterwards also conveyed to Norwich Priory. Prior to 1108 he witnessed other Charters by Henry relative to the establishment of Holy Trinity Priory, near York, as a cell of the Abbey of Marmoutier in Brittany.

He founded Sporle Priory in Norfolk as a cell of the Church of St Florent de Saumur sometime before 1122, granting the monks the Church of Sporle with its tithes, together with certain lands, twenty shillings of money yearly, wood for fire and building, and pasturage everywhere for their flocks with his own.

He married Adeliza (otherwise Adelina or Avelina), sister of Ernulph de Hesding (Picardy), the gallant defender of Shrewsbury in a later reign, and one-third of whose lands, after his barbarous execution by Stephen in 1138, came to Alan's children in right of their mother. In the Charters granted or witnessed by him he calls himself Alan Fitz-Fladald or Flaald, a designation which, from the singularity of the name, joined to other circumstances in the lives of himself and his descendants, naturally points him out as identical with that Alan Fitz-Flaald of Brittany who, in 1098, granted to the Abbey of Marmoutier the Church of Guguan or Cuguen, situated in the neighbourhood of the great castle of the Viscounts of Dinan. "Flaald," the father of the Breton "Alan," is undoubtedly identical with "Fledaldus" who, about 1097, confirmed a grant, by his brother "Alan Siniscallus" of Dol, of a site for the Abbey of Mezuoit attached to the Church of St Florent de Saumur.

According to the author of "The Norman People," writing on the authority of the Chartulary of St Florent, this grant was also confirmed by the superior of the district, Oliver, Viscount of Dinan, whose Charter is witnessed by Alan the Seneschal himself. About the same time also, Geoffry, Viscount of Dinan, granted to the same abbey certain lands near Dinan, which, as the deed bears, were part of the lands of "Alan le Seneschal, and were given with consent of Rivallon, another brother of Alan the Seneschal.

The eldest of these three brothers, about 1080 as "Alanus Siniscallus," and again in 1086 as "Alanus dapifer," witnessed charters to the same church. He engaged in the Crusade of 1097 and, dying apparently without issue, his inheritance reverted to his brother Fledald or Flaald. The third brother Rivallon or Rhiwallon became a monk, and entered the fraternity of St Florent.

The identity of Alan the son of Flaald who appears in the records of Brittany, with the Alan Fitz-Flaald who appears contemporaneously in the records of England, is conclusively proved by the Chartulary of St Florent, unless we are to believe that there were two families, one in Brittany and one in England, bearing the same names contemporaneously with each other throughout several generations, and appearing in charters of the same period in connection with the same objects.

Hitherto indeed there has been no direct evidence of the existence of Flaald in England in person, but Mr Horace Round, in his recently-published "Peerage and Family History," considers that this missing link is to be found in "Float filius Alani dapiferi" who figures as a witness to the grant of lands at Monmouth (18 March 1101 or 1102) to the Church of St Florent. Mr Round unfortunately does not indicate clearly the grounds on which he regards "Flaald" as identical with this "Float," on the strength of whose designation he assigns to Alan Fitz-Flaald Sheriff of Shropshire, a grandfather of the name of Alan. The designation in its entirety indeed indicates a son of a "dapifer" or "senescallus" of the name of Alan, but if the designation be intended to refer to the dapifer of Dol, (which, from the frequency with which the title "dapifer" appears in other connections in these old deeds, is by no means clear) then chronology would rather indicate Alan le Senescal of Dol (about 1080) as the father of this "Float"—though the connection could not have been a legitimate one—a hypothesis supported moreover by the fact that "Float's" name apparently does not emerge except in this minor capacity of a witness. The designation "dapifer" would seem a somewhat slender foundation on which to build the identity of "Float" and "Flaald," and though of course the son might easily have been an earlier immigrant than his father, and for that circumstance possibly also a much more important person in their adopted country, it must be borne in mind that "Alan the son of "Flaald" would seem to have been a landowner and religious benefactor in England considerably before 1101, while "Float," the father assigned to him by Mr Round does not appear till that year or even later and then only in a minor capacity and so far as has been yet discovered with no territorial connection.

However this may be, there is sufficient indication in the

history of Alan's descendants to prove his and their Breton origin and descent from Flaald the brother of the Crusader—Alan, Senescal of Dol in and about 1080.

The precise date of the death of Alan Sheriff of Shropshire, and nephew of the crusader in question, is uncertain—Eyton assigning it to 1114 or thereby, while Mr Round considers that this proceeds on an erroneous assumption. By his wife, Adeliza de Hesding, he left at least three sons, William, Walter, and Jordan, and a daughter, Sybil, who, about 1132, married Roger de Freville. If his son Walter was, as is now practically certain, identical with Walter, Stewart of Scotland, then he would appear to have had a fourth son Simon, who, as "brother of Walter the son of Alan," witnesses the deed of foundation of Paisley Abbey in 1164.

The first-named son, William Fitz-Alan, was in 1126 appointed by Queen Adelais, second wife of Henry I., her Sheriff or Viscount for the County of Shropshire which she had received from her husband. His descendants inherited, by marriage, the Earldom of Arundel, and changed their residence from Shropshire to Sussex, and the direct line of this branch is now represented by the Duke of Norfolk, through the marriage of Mary, only child of Henry Fitz-Alan tenth Earl of Arundel, to Thomas, fourth Duke of Norfolk, who was executed by Queen Elizabeth in 1572 for supporting the claims of Mary Queen of Scots to the English throne.

C

The recorded proofs of the existence of a Walter, son of Alan, and younger brother of William the son of Alan, have already been cited.

For the present purpose, however, the most important of Alan's sons was "Jordan," sometimes ranked as the eldest and sometimes as the youngest. He certainly appears to have heired the family estates and office of "Senescal" in Brittany, a circumstance which might indicate him as the eldest son. He also succeeded his father in lands at Burton in England, and to Mr Round's research we are indebted for the discovery that he owned the estates of Tuxford, Warsop, and others, part of the forfeited estate of Roger de Busli, in Nottinghamshire.

In 1130, "Jordan filius Alani," a valiant and illustrious man (virum strenuum et illustrem) appears, along with his wife "Mary," and his sons Jordan and Alan, in an agreement with the Abbot of Marmoutier relative to the churchyard of La Frasnais, which he had held as his by inheritance. But being made sensible that he held it wrongfully, he, anxious for his soul, at once conveyed it to the monks, together with seven and a half acres of adjoining land. The name of Jordan Fitz-Alan appears contemporaneously (1129-30) in the Pipe Rolls of England as possessed of lands in Lincolnshire.

His son, "Jordanus filius Jordani filius Alani," restored to the Church of Sele in Sussex—another cell of St Florent de Saumur—the mill at Burton which the monks had enjoyed in the time of "Alani filii Flealdi" and in the time of "Jordani, patris mei." This Jordan Fitz-Jordan seems to have died childless, as he was succeeded by his brother Alan, who, along with his wife "Joanna," and his son Jordan, appears in a deed of the time of Henry II., confirming to the monks of Lehon (Marmoutier) a grant by his grandfather, Alan Fitz-Flaald, of the tithe of his demesne at Burton. He also, as "Alanum filium quondam Jordani Dolensem Seneschallum," confirmed the grant made at Cuguen by Alan Fitz-Flaald, and bestowed on the same establishment the Church of St Mary of Tronchet or Tronquet about 1160. A Papal bull by Alexander III. (1159-1178) also shows that this Alan Fitz-Jordan Fitz-Alan—"a noble man Alan, Seneschal of Dol, son of Jordan deceased"—had given the Abbey of Tiron all his rights in the Church of Tronchet, together with all tithes of his substance which he detained in his own hands, as well as the Churches of Sharrington (in Norfolk), and Tophor, and Garsop, identified by Mr Round as Tuxford and Warsop, situated on his Nottinghamshire estates.

He figures as witness in a deed at Winchester in 1167, and in the same year in one relative to the Abbey of Vieuville, to which his wife Joan and his daughter Olive were afterwards benefactors for the repose of his soul.

His son Jordan, mentioned in his grant to Marmoutier,

seems to have died without issue, as the latter's sister, Olive, appears in possession of the family property at Sharrington in 1227. Another sister, Alicia, whose death occurs in the records of Dol, appears to have inherited the Brittany lands and office, and to have also been a benefactress to the Abbey of Vieuville.

The "Senescals of Dol" with whom we thus trace Alan Fitz-Flaald's connection are stated by the author of "The Norman People" to have been descended from the old Armorican Counts of Dol and Dinan, a race whose origin is lost in the mists of antiquity. They are generally believed to have been the descendants and representatives of the ancient patriarchal rulers of Armorica in the time of Julius Cæsar. The author already quoted, states that they were sovereigns rather than magnates; that their principality embraced a tract of over 5000 square miles of country—running from St Malo on the coast, to the central hills of Brittany—and that numerous barons were dependent on them.

They first definitely and authentically appear in recorded history about the middle of the sixth century. Frogerius, Count of Dol, is mentioned as a great magnate in the time of

Samson, Abbot of Dol (about A.D. 570). He was succeeded by Loiescan, who granted to the Abbey of Dol an estate in Jersey. Rivallon, who restored a monastery at the Abbot's request, is mentioned in the church records about 710, as "potentissmus vir." A hundred years later, mention is made of Salomon, Count of Dol, who had three sons, Rivallon, Alan, and Guigan, who about 868 witnessed a Charter by Solomon, King of Bretagne. Alan, Count of Dol, appears about 919 in connection with the marriage of his daughter to Ralph, the lord of Rieux. Another Salomon figures about 930 as "Advocate" or protector of the Church of Dol, founded by his predecessors Frogerius and Loiescan. He seems to have been succeeded by his brother Ewarin, Count of Dol—the father of "Alan, son of Ewarin," and of Gotscelin de Dinan, who, about 980, witnessed a Charter by Bertha, the mother of Duke Conan.

The similarity, and in some instances the singularity of the names, and the continuity with which they appear in successive generations, might alone be considered substantial proof of the relationship between the Brittany House of De Dinan, and the English House of Fitz-Alan, and even the Scottish House of Stewart, and the probability of relationship is strengthened by the arms borne by the three families. The importance of this form of proof has always been admitted, particularly in reference to the earlier centuries, when the use of armorial insignia was guarded with an exclusiveness and jealousy altogether foreign to later times. Of the arms of these early days too, the most characteristic and distinguishing feature was simplicity, and, without attaching undue weight or importance to the matter, it can scarcely fail to be regarded as at least singular, and a somewhat striking additional coincidence, that the similarity found in the family names should also extend to the family arms. Such, however, is the case, and the "fesse," *indented* in the case of the De Dinans of Bretagne, is perpetuated in the fesse *barry* of Fitz-Alan and Fitz-Flaald, and the fesse *chequé* of the Stewarts.

The exact period at which Flaald or his son Alan emigrated from Brittany to England has not been determined with certainty. By some writers Flaald is said to have accompanied the Conqueror to the Battle of Hastings, but his name does not appear in the Domesday Book, or in the Roll of Battle Abbey — a very incomplete list, however — or in any other list of the Conqueror's companions.

It is therefore more likely that their settlement in England took place at a later date—not improbably in the reign of Henry I., who, according to the historian Eyton, in order to strengthen his hold on the Crown to which his title was not free from challenge, displaced in many cases the former Norman counsellors, and substituted foreigners in their room. "Such," he says, "in Shropshire, were Warin

" de Metz, a Lorrainer, the three Peverils, and, greatest of
" all, Alan the Son of Flaald."

Moreover, as Mr Round indicates in his work already
quoted, Henry I., as a younger son and lord of the Côtentin,
had many Breton friends and neighbours, by whom he
was also assisted, when besieged in Mont St Michael, and
whom he appears to have rewarded by grants of English
fiefs on attaining the regal dignity. It was therefore
no doubt under Henry, that Alan Fitz-Flaald first settled in
England.

Such are the rival accounts and arguments relative to
the origin and ancestry of the House of Stewart—the one
based entirely on tradition; the other though lacking in
direct documentary proof as to the identity of the Scottish
" Walter the son of Alan " with the Shropshire Baron of
the same name—yet based on circumstantial evidence of
coincidence and co-relation only second to absolute certainty.

It is for the individual reader to decide which account
is the more worthy of credit, and some may even yet
prefer the *via media* and to follow Lord Hailes who—
writing however, it is proper to say, before the re-

searches of Chalmers and others—thus summed up the position :—

"In the reign of David I., before the middle "of the twelfth century, the family of the Stewarts was "opulent and powerful. It may therefore have existed for "many ages previous to that time, but when and what was its "commencement we cannot determine."

Passing from such speculations, the first authentic appearance of the Stewarts on the page of history is, as has been indicated, to be found in the person of Walter the son of Alan, who, under that designation, witnesses many charters, chiefly those of David I. By David he was created Stewart of Scotland,—being the first to hold that high office,—and in the grant of the office he appears in possession of the lands of Paisley, Pollock, Cathcart, Talahec, Le Drip, Le Mutrene, Eaglesham, and Lochwinnoch in Renfrewshire, and of Innerwick in East Lothian. The last-named lands were of great extent, and it may here be casually observed that the superiority of Innerwick remained with Walter's descendants till the time of Charles II. at least.

In 1157 King Malcolm IV. confirmed the honours bestowed by his predecessor David I., and made the office of Stewart of Scotland hereditary in Walter's family, granting him for his lodging and the maintenance of his rank while travelling on the King's service, a toft and 20 acres of land in every Royal burgh and on every Royal estate. Walter at this date appears as lord of the lands of Stenton in East Lothian, Legerswood and Birchenside on the Leader Water in Berwickshire, and of Hassendean in Roxburghshire, in addition to those previously

D

mentioned—his whole estates being held of the King for five knights' service.

In 1164 Walter defeated Somerled of the Isles in his descent on the Barony of Renfrew, in which invasion Somerled's son was slain. He would appear about this time, and probably in reward of his services against Somerled, to have obtained another large addition to his lands, as he is now found in possession of the whole district of Strathgryfe in Renfrewshire, and the western half of Kyle in Ayrshire, lying between the Irvine water in the north and the Ayr and Lugar waters in the south. This district of Kyle took from him the name of Walter's Kyle, and at a later date, Kyle Stewart —a designation familiar to all readers of the national bard. The other portion, known by way of distinction as King's Kyle, also came into the possession of Walter's descendants on their accession to the Crown.

During the same year, 1164, Walter founded the Abbey of Paisley, for the souls of King David, King Henry, and Earl Henry (i.e., David I. King of Scots; Henry I. King of England; and Henry, Prince of Scotland and Earl of Huntingdon), and for the salvation, body and soul, of King Malcolm, and of the Stewart himself, and all his parents, benefactors, and descendants. It was dedicated to God and the Blessed Virgin, and more particularly to St James, St Milburga, and St Mirin. St James was the special or patron saint of the Stewarts; St Milburga was the founder and patron saint of Wenlock, while St Mirin was a Celtic saint, and the first preacher of Christianity to the natives of Clydesdale. To some who regard Walter as a Norman, his choice of a Saxon and a Celtic saint has been matter of surprise, while others again see in that choice, proof of his own Saxon-Celtic descent, and of the truth of the traditionary accounts of his ancestry. The selection of patrons for his new abbey is, however, susceptible of another and possibly simpler explanation—St Milburga being the patron saint of the parent house of Wenlock and of Walter's birthplace, while St Mirin may be regarded as the patron saint of Walter's adopted home and of the district in which his abbey was situated. He endowed it munificently with thirteen churches, and numerous fishings, mills, lands, tithes, and other property. His wife, his son, and grandsons, and many other relatives and dependants followed his example, until the Abbey of Paisley became one of the wealthiest religious institutions in Scotland. There is, indeed, no other instance in history of a religious establishment so richly endowed by a single private family. It is not without a certain pathetic interest that we find that the Stewart's Charter to Paisley Abbey was granted by him at the Castle of Fotheringay in Northamptonshire (then the property of the King of Scots, and where the Stewart and the Chancellor of Scotland, a witness to the deed, seem to have been in attendance on Malcolm IV.)—a castle destined to be the scene of the execution of one of Walter's descendants, the unfortunate Mary, Queen of Scots, and to be demolished on that account by her son James VI. on succeeding to the English throne.

Although anticipating very considerably, it may here be said that at the Reformation the yearly rental of Paisley Abbey amounted to

£2468 in money,

72 chalders 4 bolls of meal,

40   ,,   11   ,,   barley,

44   ,,   1   ,,   oats,

706 stones (or nearly $4\frac{1}{2}$ tons) of cheese,

besides other miscellaneous items; while no fewer than twenty-nine churches then belonged to it.

At that epoch the whole of this wealth passed into private hands, and, by the irony of fate, into possession of a family which, though connected by various marriages with the descendants of the original benefactors, had by no means at all times shown themselves over-well disposed towards them. In 1553, Lord Claud Hamilton, a boy of ten, third son of the Duke of Chatelherault, was created Commendator of Paisley, in succession to his uncle, John Hamilton, Archbishop of St Andrews. In 1557 the whole estates of the Abbey—the pious donation of another family and other times—were diverted from the purposes of religion, for the benefit of which the Stewarts and their friends had divested themselves of them, and were converted into a temporal lordship in favour of Lord Claud Hamilton, from whom are descended the Hamilton Dukes and Earls of Abercorn, Lords Paisley, etc.

Besides his munificence to Paisley, Walter the Stewart was a liberal benefactor of the Monasteries of Kelso, Dunfermline, Cupar, and Melrose. He died in 1177, and was buried in his Abbey of Paisley, leaving a son, Alan, and a daughter, Margaret, by his wife Eschina, daughter of Thomas de Londonius,—the "Hostiarius" or Doorward under William the Lion—an office from which his descendants afterwards took the name of Durward. With this lady, Walter obtained large possessions in Roxburghshire, notably the lands of Molla and Huntlaw on the Bowmont Water.

Whether Chalmers be correct or not in assuming William FitzAlan to have been Walter's elder brother, there appears no doubt that he had a brother Simon, as, in the testing clause to the Foundation Charter of Paisley Abbey, "Simone Fratre Walteri filii Alani" appears as witnessing the deed. This Simon is believed to have been the ancestor of the Boyds (Celtic "Buidhe" or fair-haired), and it is unquestionable that the Boyds carry the same armorial bearings as the Stewarts—the "fesse chequé"—assumed by the latter in virtue of their office as Keepers of the Royal Exchequer and originating in the chequered covering, or *coopertura*, of the table on which the general accounts of the Kingdom, originally under the control of the Stewart, were computed. By means of this chequered cover, calculations were made with counters as on a chess-board, whereby, with the aid of attendant minstrels, what must at that time, for various reasons, have been a complicated and troublesome work was sought to be lightened and facilitated. It may, perhaps, be permitted to speculate whether this name "Simon" may not be a corruption, accidental or phonetic, of "Salomon," a circumstance which would, of course, furnish another striking instance of that similarity or continuity of family name to which allusion has already been made.

On his vast estates Walter encouraged the settlement of many Normans and others, whose descendants were destined in after years to play, along with his own, an important part in the history of their adopted country.

Prominent among these were the Montgomeries, whose ancestor Robert de Montgumbri obtained from his friend Walter the Stewart a grant of the barony of Eaglesham. From him descended the Earls of Eglinton, through the celebrated Sir John Montgomery, who captured Hotspur Percy at the Battle of Otterburn and with his ransom built the castle of Pulnoon.

The Lockharts of Lee trace their descent to Symon Loccard, who in 1165 held Symington (Simon's "ton," or dwelling) in Kyle, from Walter the Stewart, under whom he also held a manor in Lanarkshire, similarly named.

In Kyle also, one of the principal vassals of the Stewart

was Richard Waleys, who is believed to have founded Riccarton (Richard's "ton"), while another branch of the same family settled on the Stewart's estates in Renfrewshire, where their representative became the ancestor of Sir William Waleys or Wallace, the Scottish champion.

In Renfrewshire too, Robert de Croc, a Norman knight, obtained wide lands from the Stewart and named them after himself—Croc's "ton," or Crookston. These lands ultimately returned to the Stewarts through the marriage of the heiress with Stewart of Darnley, a descendant of this Walter.

The presence of Montgomery, a cadet of the great Shropshire Montgomeries Earls of Shrewsbury, is adduced by Chalmers as another proof of his theory of the origin of the Stewarts, and on this question of origin it seems somewhat significant that a generation or two later the Bishop of Dol should have been selected by the Pope (1182) to mediate in a dispute between William the Lion and the Bishop of Dunkeld. The rank of the disputants precludes any question of accident having governed the choice of an ambassador for so delicate a mission, and as, where William was concerned—a man who had defied the Pontiff's immediate predecessor—a friend at Court would be as valuable to a Pope's envoy as to a humbler suitor, the selection of the Bishop of Dol may not unwarrantably be placed with the other arguments for the descent of William's chief Officer of State from the ancient Counts of Dol.

Walter the Stewart was succeeded in his office and estates by his son Alan, who is said to have been present with his father at the overthrow of Somerled, and to have been thus early initiated in war. Along with David, Earl of Huntingdon, Prince of Scotland, he accompanied Richard Cœur de Lion and Philip of France to the Holy War, and was present at the siege of Ptolemais in 1191. Returning to Scotland he suppressed a rebellion in Morayshire—the leader of which, Roderick, the son of Harold Earl of Caithness, fell by the Stewart's sword, in a sanguinary engagement near Inverness.

He appears to have emulated his father in his acts of piety,—his donations to Paisley, Kelso, Cupar, Melrose, and other religious communities being numerous and extensive.

He greatly extended the family possessions,—the Island of Bute appearing in his hands before 1200,—while by his wife Eva, daughter of Swan, son of Thor, Lord of Tippermuir and Tranent, he obtained a further increase of territory. He died in 1204, and was buried with great pomp in Paisley Abbey.

Alan left two sons, Walter his successor, and David, who appears as a guarantor of King Alexander's engagement to marry the Princess of England. Of David's descendants, if any, history has however preserved no account.

Walter, third hereditary High Stewart of Scotland, is known also by the territorial designation of "de Dundonald," and it was he, moreover, who first settled the name of Stewart on his posterity. Surnames only came into general use about this time. Many families adopted or continued as a surname their old territorial or landed designation, such as Douglas, Menteith, Crawford, Ruthven, and the like, but Walter chose the title of his office, by which he and his ancestors had been known for over a century. It has pleased some vendors of cheap witticisms to be merry at the expense of this selection of a name, arguing that, etymologically considered, the word implies "Keeper of the hogs"! (Saxon, "Sti" and "ward"). "Sti," a dwelling, is of course capable of application both to the shelter of hogs and of their owners, and, moreover, as hogs were a principal source of wealth among the Saxons, it may even be that, in earlier days, the duties of the "Stiward," or Housemaster, extended to the care of the stock as well as to the house, of his lord. It is scarcely necessary, however, to point out that, even if this were once so, the word had lost all such significance long before this family were Stewards of Scotland, or had adopted the surname ; and that the High Stewards of Scotland were Stewards, not to a private individual or estate, but to the sovereign, and of the royal revenues and domains. A cynic indeed might trace a peculiar appropriateness in the suggested significance of the name, in the experiences of some of the later Stewarts with

E

their subjects, but there is certainly none whatever in relation to the duties of their ancestors, the High Stewards of Scotland.

The orthography of the name has been equally canvassed and disputed. The proper form, according to modern ideas, would, in the circumstances of its adoption, be Steward; but, as usual in the Scots dialect, the hard "d" was early softened into "t," and, as "Stewart of Scotland," even the hereditary office itself is almost invariably spelt by old writers. This form has accordingly been retained throughout these notes. The substitution of "u" for "w" and the omission of the "e" are traceable to the old Scots league with France. The Stewarts of Darnley, ancestors of the Earls and Dukes of Lennox, early obtained a territorial settlement in and connection with France (as Lords D'Aubigny, etc.), where the name, owing to the absence of the letter "w" in the French alphabet, was necessarily spelt "u." The form "Stuart" was thus introduced and continued by that family and its cadets, and, later, by Queen Mary on her return from France. The form "Steuart" adopted by the Steuarts of Allanton and their cadets is simply a compromise between the original and the new method, and is likewise traceable to a connection with France. With these exceptions the orthographical form follows no rule. Queen Mary's example, no doubt, accounts for the adoption of the form "Stuart" by many families, it being doubt-less considered fashionable, then as now, to follow the Royal lead. From this circumstance, too, an opinion prevails in some quarters that this form "Stuart" denotes descent from the Royal line, but the instances quoted of the Darnley and Allanton branches—descended from the High Stewards before the family succeeded to the throne, and who yet were the first to introduce these innovations—disprove this theory. Indeed, Queen Mary's son, James VI., with the pedantry which distinguished him in so many small matters, was one of the strongest opponents of the innovation, and insisted on the original form "Stewart" being retained in official documents. Similarly, while the Earls of Galloway, descended from a common ancestor with the Stuarts of Darnley and Steuarts of Allanton, retain the original spelling, "Stewart," the Blantyre family, descended from the Galloway line, have adopted the form "Stuart." Other instances might be given, but probably sufficient has been said to show that the precise orthographic form is largely a matter of individual taste, and that when speaking generically of the race as a whole, the proper spelling is the original "Stewart," while the form adopted by individual families should be followed when referring to them.

Leaving the history of the name and returning once more to that of the race, we find Walter, the third hereditary Stewart of Scotland, high in favour with his sovereign, who employed him both in love and war. In his youth Walter is said to have been also engaged in the Crusades, and to have led a command to the Holy War. Returning to Scotland he was, in 1230, appointed by Alexander II., Justiciar of Scotland in addition to his hereditary office of Stewart. To him the King entrusted the negotiations for the Royal marriage with Mary, daughter of Ingelram de Coucy, and to the Justiciar was also committed the task of suppressing a serious rising of the Galwegians.

On the death, in 1234, of Alan, Constable of Scotland, and last of the ancient Lords of Galloway, his vast estates and noble offices and titles devolved, in the absence of lawful male issue, on three daughters, all married to Englishmen. The customs of Galloway being opposed to female succession in such matters, the Galwegians petitioned the King to take the Lordship of Galloway into his own hands, or alternatively, to confer it on the late lord's natural son, Thomas. King Alexander, however, declined to entertain their request, whereupon the Galwegians rose in rebellion, in support of the pretensions of Thomas. The three ladies being descended of the blood royal, the King in person marched an army into Galloway to uphold their rights, but though he succeeded in defeating the rebels, no sooner had he retired than the rebellion again broke out. Walter, High Stewart and Justiciar of Scotland—whose daughter, it may be said, was married to Nigel or Neil, Earl of Carrick, a cousin of the three heiresses of Galloway—was thereupon sent to suppress this fresh rebellion, a task in which he effectually succeeded.

In his dual capacity of Stewart and Justiciar of Scotland,

Walter must have been possessed of vast influence and power, which a semi-royal alliance tended to consolidate and increase. He married Beatrix, the daughter of Gilchrist Earl of Mar and of his wife Marjorie, daughter of Henry Prince of Scotland, brother of Kings Malcolm IV. and William IV. In the veins of Walter's descendants therefore, flowed the blood of the ancient Kings of Scotland, whose crown was destined, through another royal alliance four generations later, to adorn the brows of the Stewart's heir.

Like his father and grandfather, Walter the Stewart was a liberal benefactor of the Church, not the least interesting of his benefactions being a gift of six chalders of meal annually to the monks of Paisley to support a priest to pray for the soul of Robert de Brus, Lord of Annandale, who died in 1245—an early instance of the friendship and close association existing between the families of Brus and Stewart. Walter died in 1246, a year after his friend Brus, leaving five sons and three daughters. The latter were—Elizabeth, who married Malduin, Earl of Lenox; Christian (or, according to some writers, Euphemia), wife of Patrick, Earl of Dunbar; and Margaret, married, as already stated, to Neil, Earl of Carrick, whose daughter Marjory, Countess of Carrick in her own right, married Robert de Brus, Lord of Annandale, and thus became mother of the celebrated Robert de Brus, King of Scots.

Walter's sons were, Alexander, his successor; Sir Robert

of Tarbolton and Crookston, or Crocston; John, Walter, and William.

Of John all that is known is that he accompanied his brothers Alexander and Walter, and his brother-in-law Patrick, Earl of Dunbar, to the Crusades, and fell at the Battle of Damietta in 1248—his brother-in-law of Dunbar sharing the same fate.

William, the youngest son, is believed to have been ancestor of the Ruthvens, as, in authentic documents, "William de Ruthven" is designated "son of Walter, son of Alan the son-in-law of Thor"—a pedigree, it will be observed, which applies to all the family of Walter, third hereditary Stewart of Scotland.

Walter's remaining son, named after himself Walter, was the ancestor of the Menteiths, and figures in his country's history with almost equal prominence to his eldest brother, Alexander, and his history and that of his descendants can best and most conveniently be outlined here before continuing the story of the main line.

In his youth Walter Stewart, son of Walter, the third who held the hereditary office, accompanied his brothers Alexander and John and his brother-in-law the Earl of Dunbar, to the Holy War. On his return he married Mary Comyn, younger daughter of Walter Comyn, Earl of Menteith. Her elder sister, Isabella, had succeeded to the estates and honours of her father, but fell into disgrace, being suspected of poisoning her husband Sir William Comyn. Shortly after his death she, with indecent haste, married Sir John Russell, described as an "ignoble English knight," and having failed to ask or obtain the consent of the Crown (of which she was a ward) to this marriage, she was imprisoned, stripped of her lands and dignities, and compelled to seek shelter in England. The Menteith honours and estates were thereupon claimed by Walter Stewart in right of his wife Mary, co-heiress with the banished Countess. The claim was allowed, and Walter thereupon became Earl of Menteith in accordance with the old Scots law as to transmission of dignities in such cases.

The exiled Countess, however, succeeded in obtaining the sympathy of Rome, and in 1262 Pope Urban IV. sent a Nuncio, Pontius, to York and arrogantly called on Walter Stewart for an explanation. The Pontiff's right to interfere in secular matters was however denied in the most spirited manner by King Alexander II., who declined to permit any such intervention in the affairs of his kingdom.

The next year (1263) witnessed the great Danish invasion of Scotland, to repel which Walter Stewart, Earl of Menteith, marched his retainers to the assistance of King Alexander and his brother, Alexander the Stewart.

In 1271 he appears as Sheriff of Dumbarton, and two years later he was again called on to defend his title and lands from a new opponent in the person of John Comyn of Badenoch, the chief of the powerful house of Comyn, and who, as tutor and guardian for his son William who had married the daughter of the exiled Countess Isabella, now claimed the earldom of Menteith for his son and daughter-in-law. The controversy dragged on for twelve years, during which Comyn attempted to transfer the trial to the jurisdiction of England. King Alexander, however, once more displayed his resolution not to suffer any foreign interference in the affairs of Scotland, and Comyn's attempt failed. The case was at length settled by Alexander and his Parliament dividing the lands between the rival claimants, but confirming the dignity of the earldom to Walter Stewart and his heirs.

In 1288 the Earl of Menteith and his Countess travelled to Norway in the suite of the Princess Margaret of Scotland, and attended her marriage with Eric, King of Norway, and also her subsequent coronation. Returning to Scotland he again appears as Sheriff of Dumbarton in 1289, and when, on the death of the Maid of Norway, Edward of England endeavoured to establish a title as Lord Paramount of Scotland, the Earl of Menteith, in common with all the other Scots Lords, recognised for the time being a claim which they were at the moment powerless to oppose. On the trial of the rival claims of Baliol and Brus to the Scottish Crown in 1291, Walter, Earl of Menteith, was appointed by Brus to act as one of his auditors or representatives before King Edward, and on that monarch giving the award against Brus, the Earl of Menteith declined to countenance Baliol's title or appear at his coronation. The next few years of Walter's life are involved in obscurity, and history appears to have confused him with his son Alexander, and again with Sir John Graham, the husband of his great grand-daughter, who in her right was Earl of Menteith. According to the early writers, Walter Stewart, Earl of Menteith, was captured at Dunbar in 1296, and executed by orders of King Edward. Later research, however, points to his son Alexander as being the Earl of Menteith captured at Dunbar, and to Sir John Graham being the Earl of Menteith executed by orders of Edward—third of the name, however, instead of first. This theory is further supported by the fact that in 1296 Walter Stewart, Earl of Menteith, would have been nearly eighty years of age —an unlikely age for the leading of raiders into England and the defence of Border castles, and equally unlikely to provoke

F

Edward's resentment at least to the extent of the penalty of death. The probability therefore is that Walter, Earl of Menteith, died about 1294, predeceased by his Countess, and was buried in the Priory of Inchmahome, in the lake of Menteith, amid the ruins of which still stands their tomb where—

"The steel clad Stewart, red cross knight
"Menteith, his countess fair and bright,
"Live here in sculptured stone."

The tomb displays the recumbent figures of the Earl and of his wife, whose arm encircles her husband's neck. The knight's legs are crossed, indicating the crusader, and his shield bears his paternal arms,—the "fesse chequé," for Stewart, differenced with a label of five points as a cadet of the principal stem of Stewart.

By his wife, the Countess Mary Comyn, Walter—who was also known by the soubriquet of "Bailloch" or "the freckled"—left two sons, Alexander who succeeded him, and Sir John "de Menteith," who obtained his father's lands of Knapdale in Argyllshire, and is celebrated in popular history as the betrayer of Wallace—a reputation which, as will be seen, is as undeserved as the foundation of the legend is false.

As the Menteith honours did not long remain in this branch of the Stewarts, it may be convenient to follow out here the history of those two brothers, before resuming the story of the main line.

The elder, Alexander, Earl of Menteith after his father's death, took an active part with the national party against King Edward on the breaking out of the War of Independence in 1295. Along with other Scots nobles he entered England, ravaged Cumberland, and besieged Carlisle. In the following year, 1296, he was sent along with the Earls of Athol and Ross to take over the Castle of Dunbar, which the Countess of Dunbar in the absence of her husband, Earl " Patrick with the black beard," had offered to place under the Scots Estates. In this mission he was accompanied by his brother, Sir John Menteith,—an important circumstance in considering the latter's career,—and both brothers fell into Edward's hands at this time. No sooner had that monarch learned of the surrender of Dunbar, than he dispatched an army against it under the Earl of Surrey. The Scots Estates likewise sent an army to the assistance of the garrison, but these troops being entirely defeated, the three Earls and their followers had no alternative but to surrender.

The old Scots historians, as has already been indicated, ascribe this transaction to Walter, the first Stewart Earl of Menteith, and proceed to relate that King Edward ordered him to immediate execution. Lord Hailes was the first writer to cast doubt on this version, and though Tytler and other later historians have accused him of seeking to whitewash the character of Edward, subsequent research has proved his lordship's surmise to have been correct. Documents have recently been discovered which had apparently been drawn up for signature by the captive earls as a condition of their freedom, and in which they were to swear fealty to Edward and grant hostages for their future good behaviour. One of these, dated at Elgin soon after the Battle of Dunbar, runs in the name of "Alexander, Earl of Menteith," and though—as it was never signed by the Earl, and as his father *might* also have been present and *might* have been executed as alleged—it cannot be absolutely conclusive evidence against the old story, it yet certainly points to the probability of Walter's death before 1296, and to Alexander being the Earl of Menteith referred to in the transactions of the years 1295 and 1296. Alexander, doubtless owing to the mediation of his friends, Brus and Dunbar, then with Edward, does not seem to have been long kept a prisoner, as, after giving his two sons Alan and Peter, as hostages, he was released and took an oath of fealty to Edward in August 1296. His brother, Sir John Menteith, appears to have been more obstinate or patriotic, as he did not obtain his freedom till long afterwards and on entirely different conditions. Earl Alexander cannot long have survived his release, as his son Alan appears in possession of the Earldom in 1303. In addition to Alan and Peter delivered as hostages to Edward in 1296, Alexander left other two sons Murdach and Alexander. The two hostages accompanied the English monarch to the French wars, as is proved by the entries in the records of England relative to the expense for horses and armour which Edward presented to them before setting out. On this expedition also they were accompanied by their uncle, Sir John Menteith.

Of Peter and Alexander nothing more is known. Alan, on his return to Scotland succeeded his father in the Earldom of Menteith, which he certainly possessed in 1303. He was one of the first to join Bruce, on the latter raising the standard of independence, but had the misfortune to be made prisoner early in the war. His estates and titles were thereupon forfeited by King Edward, who conferred them on Sir John de Hastings, by whom they had been claimed in right of his mother, Isabella Comyn—the same lady who had originally married her cousin Sir William Comyn, and opposed Walter, the first Stewart Earl of Menteith, in the enjoyment of his new dignities. After her former husband's death, Isabella married Sir Edmund Hastings, to whom she had two sons, Sir John and Sir Edmund. The elder brother, who originally obtained from King Edward the grant of the Scottish Earldom of Menteith, would appear to have conveyed it to his brother, Sir Edmund, as the latter appears in the English records of the time as "Dominus de Enchinchelmok," or "Enchimelmok," while his seal bears the inscription, "S: Edmundi: Hasting: Comitatv: Menetei." These barbarous designations have greatly puzzled the English antiquarians. "The Comitatv: Menetei," they think, may be intended to indicate "St David's in Wales"! But the uncouth "Enchinchelmok" they can by no means fathom. The late Mr John Riddell, the well-known authority on Scots Peerage Law, solves the difficulty, however, by proving the Hastings-Comyn-Menteith connection, and thereby indicating the probability, if not indeed the certainty, that "Comitatv: Menetei" simply meant "Comitatus" (or Earldom) of "Menteith," while the "Dominus de Enchinchelmok" was nothing more than the attempted English rendering of Dominus (or Lord) of Inchmahome, or as it was written of old, "Inchmaquhomok," the larger of two islands in the Lake of Menteith, on which stand the ruins of the ancient Priory built by the Comyns, the original Earls of Menteith.

Of Earl Alan (Stewart) of Menteith little more is known except that he left a son (who died young) and a daughter. The forfeiture of his friend was of course ignored by Brus, and it is certain that Hastings can never have had more than a nominal possession of the lands. On the death of Earl Alan's son, the Earldom, by arrangement with Brus, passed to Murdach, brother of the deceased Earl Alan. Like his brother, the new Earl had thrown in his lot with Brus, and his services had already been rewarded by grants of the lands of Dalmeny and Barnbougle in Linlithgowshire, and various others forfeited by the families of Soulis, Comyn, etc. On the usurpation of the Crown by the younger Baliol after Brus's death, Earl Murdach took up arms in support of the cause of his benefactor's infant son, David II. He was present at the disastrous Battle of Dupplin Muir in 1332, where a powerful Scots army was, owing to the incapacity of the Regent, utterly defeated by Baliol's greatly inferior force. The Scottish army was taken by surprise, and would have been entirely routed but for the exertions of the Earl of Menteith, Randolph, Earl of Moray, Robert Brus Earl of Carrick, Alexander Fraser, and other Barons, who, rallying their followers, charged the enemy, and, for the time, saved the situation. Encouraged, however, by the inferiority of the enemy's forces, discovered by the increasing daylight, the Regent launched horse and foot against them in a manner, which, as in the case of Bannockburn, worked the destruction of the numerically superior force. Pressing on each other in headlong confusion, the Scottish soldiers endeavoured to reach the enemy. Many were trampled upon by their own friends, and the undisciplined mass fell an easy prey to the steady courage of Baliol's troops. A dreadful carnage ensued, in which the brave Earl Murdach and others of the Scots nobility perished, and many more were made prisoners. Some historians relate that Murdach was not killed but only made prisoner, and having subsequently escaped, rejoined the Scottish army, and accompanied the new Regent, Douglas, to Halidon Hill, and fell there in 1333. But this version is opposed to the generally accepted view.

On Earl Murdach's death, without issue, the Earldom of Menteith reverted to his niece Mary, the daughter of his brother Alan. The young Countess married Sir John Graham of Kincardine, to whom she had one daughter, also Mary, who succeeded to the Earldom of Menteith, married her relative Robert Stewart, Duke of Albany and Regent of Scotland during the minority of King James I., and thus brought the Menteith honours into the main line of the Stewarts.

Her father, Sir John Graham, Earl of Menteith in right of his wife, was, as previously indicated, captured at the Battle of Durham in 1346, and executed by order of Edward III. It is this incident which, it seems probable, gave rise in course of time to the story of Walter Stewart, Earl of Menteith, having been made prisoner at Dunbar, and executed by order of Edward I. The similarity in the names of the battles, the titles of the victims, and of the executioners, no doubt confused historians writing at a later period and with imperfect information, and thus Walter Stewart, Earl of Menteith, believed to have been taken prisoner at the Battle of Dunbar by Edward I., was confounded with Sir John Graham, Earl of Menteith, captured at Durham by Edward III., and by that monarch ordered to be executed.

Few characters in history have been so much maligned, their virtues so much concealed, and their name consigned to so much unmerited obloquy, as Sir John Menteith, the second son of Walter, the first Stewart Earl of Menteith.

What Scotsman or Scotswoman has not heard of the "false Menteith," the betrayer of Wallace, a man guilty of one of the vilest and basest deeds,—treachery to a friend who trusted his life to his honour? So deeply rooted is this conception of the man, that it is difficult to credit the fact that there is absolutely no evidence to warrant it, and on the contrary, much to contradict and disprove it.

The charge against Menteith is that he had been the especial friend and colleague of Wallace, and that after thus associating and making common cause with him against the common enemy,—the English,—he deserted his country and meanly betrayed the confiding Wallace into the hands of the relentless Edward. The sole authority for the charge is "Blind Harry," a wandering minstrel, whose history is proved to be full of inaccuracies; whom, as Lord Hailes says, every historian copies, but whom none will venture to quote as an authority.

As regards the alleged friendship between Wallace and

G

Menteith, the only attempt which has been made even to show them engaged together on the same enterprise, is in connection with the well-known "burning of the barns of Ayr," and the account is so conflicting and, in many respects, so utterly opposed to other well-known facts, as to be altogether unworthy of credit or acceptance as affording any proof of the alleged friendship. Lord Hailes, a historian "superior to most "men in the relevancy of his deductions, and in the power "and acuteness of his criticism," and one whose surmises and theories even are more valuable, and better worth attention, than the alleged facts of some other writers, was the first to reject, or at least to doubt Blind Harry's tale; and in this, as in other questions, later enquiries have proved how well-founded his Lordship's opinion has been, and how unjustifiable also are the attacks made on his Lordship himself because, in his respect for the truth and his refusal to condemn the innocent without due proof of guilt, he deviated from accepted tradition and popular ideas in this matter.

The facts of Sir John Menteith's life as now ascertained are these, and an impartial consideration will show them to be entirely at variance with the legendary tale transmitted by "Blind Harry."

Sir John was, as we have seen, taken prisoner by Edward I. along with his brother Alexander, Earl of Menteith, at the capture of Dunbar in 1296. The English records show that he was detained a close prisoner until August of the following year 1297, as accounts for his maintenance and guarding are still extant. At that date he was brought to the presence of Edward, and apparently offered his freedom if he would join his service. This he declined to do so far as Scotland was concerned, but he agreed to accompany Edward in his projected expedition to France. To this expedition Edward's barons were bitterly opposed, and he therefore appears to have beat up recruits among his Scottish prisoners, several of whom, as a condition of freedom, agreed to accompany him thither, while declining to assist him in Scotland. The expedition sailed in 1297, and did not return until the following year 1298, and it is therefore clear that as Sir John Menteith was in the hands of King Edward from 1296 to 1298, he had, during that period at least, no opportunity of making even the acquaintance, much less the *friendship* of Wallace, who, it should be kept in mind, only came into notice early in 1297, and whose prominence as the leader of the Scottish patriots lasted less than two years altogether. After the disastrous Battle of Falkirk in July 1298, Edward, as is well known, overran Scotland, and Wallace, relinquishing the Governorship, retired into comparative obscurity. During the next few years the government of the country was practically in Edward's hands, and in 1303 Sir John Menteith, apparently bowing to the inevitable, accepted the Constableship of Dumbarton Castle and the Sheriffdom of the county from the ruling power. It is not improbable that in the expedition to France in which he accompanied Edward, he may even have conceived some regard for that monarch's better qualities, and thus have been more easily reconciled to accept employment under him. However that may be, the fact that Edward entrusted this important castle to him seems to disprove any connection on the part of Sir John Menteith with Wallace, as it is almost inconceivable that Edward should have placed in a position of such trust any one who had recently been in arms against himself, and still less so that he should have confided so much to anyone known or supposed to be a special friend of Wallace, whom he rightly regarded as the mainspring and centre of all opposition to his power. Conversely it is as Lord Hailes remarks, equally "improbable that Wallace should " have put himself in the power of a man whom he knew to be " in an office of such distinguished trust with Edward." That monarch, as is well known, had never forgiven Wallace, whose career, though short, had occasioned him so much trouble, and had practically blasted his chance of ever ruling over Scotland. Consequently he left no means untried to effect his capture, and the English records show that he liberated many Scottish prisoners on condition that they would "labour to take William Waleys." Among those so liberated were Sir John Comyn, Sir Alexander Lindsay, Sir David Graham, and Sir Simon Fraser, who had been con-demned to exile, and who now secured their freedom on such shameful conditions. Some of these knights certainly never meant to keep their word, and paid the penalty with their life—as in the case of Sir Simon Fraser—when they fell into Edward's hands at a later stage. Other prisoners were released at various times on similar terms, and notably, reference is made in the English records of these transactions to a page or valet who was considered most likely to effect Edward's purpose.

These machinations were at length successful, and Wallace having been taken prisoner, was handed over by his captors to the governor of the district, Sir John Menteith, by whom he was transmitted to Edward. That Menteith was not the man who betrayed him is further evident from original papers relative to the business of the English Council of the day, wherein there appear entries as to rewards to be given of " 40 " marks to the valet who spied out William Waleys," and other 60 marks to be divided between the others who were present at his capture. If these entries stood alone, there might still be room for surmise that, however improbable, Sir John Menteith may have been the "*valet* who spied out William Waleys," or, at least, that he was among those "present at his capture." Both doubts are however removed by a subsequent entry in the same notes "of 100 livres to Sir John de Menteith." No explanation is given as to the circumstances in which this sum was paid, but the entry at least disproves the tale that Menteith was the betrayer or was present at the capture of Wallace—separate payments having already been made to others for their services in these connections. The silence of the records as to the circumstances of the larger payment, of course leaves it open to suspicion of having possibly been in some way connected with Wallace, but in that case it is at least singular that the records should have been so particular as to the nature and circumstances of the smaller payments, and altogether mute as to the larger one, which, if a reward, must surely have been for a still more valuable and meritorious service, and one which might have been expected to be considered still more worthy of being placed on record. The probability is however that it was simply payment of an account rendered by Sir John Menteith in connection with his governorship of Dumbarton, possibly even the expense of guarding and transmitting Wallace to London. The three entries taken together certainly disprove the popular story of Wallace having been either betrayed or captured by Sir John Menteith, and an impartial consideration of these facts, together with the previous career of Sir John Menteith, seems to prove that any connection he had with Wallace, whatever it might be, must have been confined to his official capacity of Constable of Dumbarton Castle. The facts connected with Sir John's prolonged imprisonment and absence from Scotland conclusively prove that there could have been, as Lord Hailes surmised, "no intercourse of familiarity or friendship" between them during Wallace's brief struggle for the independence of his country—a fact sufficient in itself to refute the entire calumny. It is also clear that Sir John Menteith cannot truly or reasonably be said to have "deserted his country" in the sense of the allegation made against him, since his imprisonment during practically the whole period of the struggle precluded his having taken up arms for it. To the extent of accepting the governorship of Dumbarton he may be so accused, but it must be remembered that at that time, and until Brus's outbreak three years later, there was no real or lasting opposition to Edward's authority. That Menteith certainly was not the traitor himself is proved by the English records quoted, and though it is beyond doubt that Wallace was brought to him as governor of the district in which the capture took place, and was by him transmitted to Edward, it will be admitted that that is a very different position and a very different share in Wallace's misfortunes from that generally assigned him.

It may be said that a patriotic Scot might have found means of permitting his prisoner's escape. But that by no means follows. The garrison under Menteith appears to have consisted of English troops, as the English account of Wallace's capture is "per *milites regis in Scotia* captus est." Consequently, even had Menteith been desirous, he probably would have found no opportunity of carrying his wishes into effect. Moreover, some writers conceive it possible that, far from being a friend of Wallace, Sir John Menteith considered that he had reason to be his enemy, as largely responsible for the death of his cousin, Sir John Stewart of Bonkyl, at the Battle of Falkirk in 1298. At that battle, as will be seen later, Sir John Stewart was deserted by the other Scottish leaders, Comyn and Wallace, left to sustain the whole English attack, and, overwhelmed by numbers, perished along with most of his followers.

The whole truth of the matter seems to be that popular opinion demanded a sacrifice to the manes of the dead hero, and Sir John Menteith as governor of, and representative of the English power in, the district in which Wallace was captured, offered the easiest and most convenient victim. So far from being the renegade and dishonourable man of Blind Harry's tale, Sir John Menteith's whole career shows him to have been a man of the highest principles and most patriotic aspirations. While nearly all the Scots nobility of his time repeatedly took oaths of allegiance to Edward only to break them as soon and as often as might be convenient, Sir John Menteith alone seems to have had a higher conception of the sanctity of an oath. His name, alone of all his family, and indeed of all the barons of Scotland, is not to be found on the Ragman Roll, or lists of those who swore fealty to Edward, preferring, as has been shown, to purchase his freedom by exile rather than by a servile acknowledgment of the English power, thus disdaining what the heroic Brus, Douglas, Stewart, and others did not scruple to perform.

But, later, having given his oath, he, unlike them again, kept it, even to an enemy, and while Edward I. lived, Sir John Menteith remained faithful to his word, notwithstanding that, as his subsequent career proves, this course must have been repugnant to his real sentiments, which were highly patriotic. No sooner however did the death of Edward I. absolve him from his oath to that monarch, than Sir John threw in his lot with Brus, joined his cause when that cause looked blackest, and adhered loyally to his fortunes.

That he enjoyed the entire confidence of Brus is evident from the missions on which he employed him and the rewards he bestowed on him. In 1309 he was sent, along with Sir Neil Campbell, the king's brother-in-law, to conclude a truce with England. In 1310 he is described in an English deed as "the King's rebel," and his lands of Knapdale were bestowed by Edward II. on John, the son of Suienus de Ergadia—*when he could get possession of them.* At the Battle of Bannockburn Sir John greatly distinguished himself, and was rewarded by Brus by a grant of lands in Kintyre.

In 1315 he accompanied Randolph in the expedition to Ireland, and again, in the following year, on one of those raids in which that leader constantly ravaged the North of England. And here his traducers have to reconcile such companionship on the part of Randolph—whom they themselves describe as "loving honour and loyalty, hating falsehood " above all things, and ever fond of having the bravest knights

H

" about him, whom he dearly loved "—with one whom they would have us believe a perjured and dishonoured knight, worthy of eternal infamy for one of the basest acts of which a human being can be capable—" betrayal under tryst."

Such however was not Randolph's estimate of his friend Sir John Menteith, nor would Brus have conferred on so debased a man such a signal mark of royal esteem and favour as the grant of part of the Royal Arms of Scotland and of the Royal Tressure, as an accession to his paternal bearings. This fact is proved by seals still extant in the charter-chests of Sir John's descendants, the Earls of Mar, and the same archives show that Brus's approval did not rest here, as in 1316 he conferred on him the lands of Glen Breryche and Aulesai in Kintyre.

As tutor for his nephews, Alan and Murdach, then in minority, Sir John Menteith, as representing the Earldom of Menteith, signed the famous letter of the Scottish barons to the Pope in 1320, protesting the independence of their country and the sovereignty of Brus. Three years later, when Edward II. had been compelled to recognise and admit that independence and sovereignty, Sir John Menteith was one of the Conservators of Peace appointed in terms of the Treaty of Berwick in 1323. He is believed to have died shortly after this event, as he appears no more in history. Sir John married Elene de Mar, daughter of Gratney, Earl of Mar and his wife Christian Brus, sister of King Robert the

Brus. By his wife, Elene de Mar, Sir John had at least one son and two daughters. The son (also by name Sir John), was Lord of Arran and Knapdale, and married Katherine ——, a fact attested by a charter in which he granted certain lands to the Abbey of Kilwinning in 1357 for the safety of his own soul and that of his late wife Katherine, "Katherine "quondam sponse meæ." He seems to have left no male issue, as the lineal representation of the Earldom of Mar devolved subsequently on his mother's representatives, and was adjudged to his niece, Janet Keith wife of Thomas, Lord Erskine, and daughter of his eldest sister Christian Menteith, who had married Sir Edward Keith, to whom she had an only daughter, the above Lady Janet Erskine. In this way the Earldom of Mar passed into the family of the Erskines, the present possessors, in right of descent from Elene de Mar and Sir John Menteith. Further evidence of the descent is found in an Exchequer Roll of the time of King James I. (who insisted on the production of all titles to annuities, etc., a fact to which we are doubtless indebted for this new proof), in which £100 is paid to the wife of Sir Thomas Erskine *in her own right*, out of the fishings and fermes of Aberdeen, "per excambium terrarum de *Arane*." The grant descended to her son and heir, Sir Robert Erskine, and invariably bears to be paid in consideration of the above excambion. Sir John's second daughter, Joanna, married Malise, Earl of Strathern, but must not be confounded with another wife of that earl

(Mary —— by name), who was implicated in the Soulis conspiracy against Brus. Joanna, Countess of Strathern, lived till 1361 at least, but appears to have left no descendants. The Menteiths of Rusky, from whom descended the Haldanes of Gleneagles and the Napiers of Merchiston, sprung from Sir Walter Menteith of Rusky, who in or about 1331-2 received a grant of the lands of Rusky from Murdach, Earl of Menteith, but of whose parentage—sometimes ascribed to Sir John Menteith—there is no direct proof.

Returning from what may appear somewhat of a digression, the story of the main line of the Stewarts is resumed in the person of Alexander, fourth hereditary High Stewart of Scotland, and uncle of the said Sir John Menteith. He was born in 1214, and is also designated as "de Dundonald." Along with his brothers John and Walter and the Earl of Dunbar, his brother-in-law, he attended St Louis of France to the Holy War, and after the death of the Earl of Dunbar, commanded the Scots pilgrims.

On his return to Scotland he found the country broken up by faction consequent on the death of the king, Alexander II. The powerful family of the Comyns headed the so-called national party, and had seized the persons of the young king and queen, while two of their lords, Robert de Ross and John de Baliol, had assumed the name of Regents. To counteract the treasonable practices of this confederacy, the Stewart and his brother Walter, Earl of Menteith; his brother-in-law Neil, Earl of Carrick; his nephew Patrick, Earl of Dunbar; and his friend Robert de Brus, Lord of Annandale, joined the party of Henry III. of England, the Queen's father. In this they were supported by Alan Durward, Justiciar of Scotland, Malise Earl of Strathern, and other leading men, the object being—not to subserviate their country to Henry, but, with his support, to break the power and crush for ever the increasing strength and importance of the Comyns. Such a powerful coalition proved too much even for the Comyns, then by far the greatest family in Scotland, and in 1255 new Regents were appointed, among whom were Robert de Brus and the Stewart, and to them and other lords, King Henry undertook to deliver any Prince or Princess who might be born during the stay of his daughter Margaret, the young Queen of Scots, at his Court.

In 1263 Alexander the Stewart commanded the right wing of the Scottish army at the Battle of Largs—the left being under the leadership of his nephew Patrick, Earl of Dunbar. To that victory, in which the Norsemen under Haco were completely routed, the Stewart and his brother Walter, Earl of Menteith, contributed in no small degree, as after defeating the left wing of the Norse army, they fell upon the rear of the enemy's main body and materially assisted King Alexander to whom that part of the Danish army was immediately opposed. By the King's orders the Stewart and his brother pursued the enemy into the Western Isles and to the Isle of Man, which they compelled them to surrender and evacuate, and which were then reannexed to the Scottish Crown. Thus the Battle of Largs, though unimportant as regards the actual numbers engaged, had a most important after effect on the history and affairs of Scotland, as the spirit engendered in the Scottish army by this success, influenced by the skill and valour of the Stewarts, was undoubtedly the means of establishing the supremacy of Scotland over the Western Isles. In the same year, and no doubt in recognition of these services, the Stewart received from Alexander III. a grant of the Barony of Garlies in Galloway, which lands, it may here be said, he conveyed to his second son, Sir John Stewart of Bonkyl, in whose family they still remain in the person of the Earl of Galloway, descended from this Alexander, High Stewart of Scotland, in an unbroken male line. During this year also (1263) Alexander III. sent the Stewart to the Court of Henry III. of England to demand from that monarch the arrears of the dowry which Henry had promised to pay on his daughter's marriage with the King of Scots. In 1281 Alexander appears as one of the guarantors of the contract of marriage between the Princess Margaret of Scotland and Eric, King of Norway; and, as has already been said, his brother, the Earl of Menteith, was one of the Scots lords who accompanied the Princess to Norway, and witnessed her marriage and coronation.

Like his predecessors, Alexander's gifts to the Church were many and liberal. He married Jean, heiress of James, Lord of Bute, and died in 1283, leaving two sons, James his successor, and John (known in history as Sir John Stewart of Bonkyl), and a daughter Elizabeth, married to Sir William Douglas of Lugton, near Dalkeith. Some writers say that he left a third son, Andrew, but of this there is no proof.

James, fifth hereditary High Stewart, was born about 1243, and is said to have joined the Earls of Carrick, Athole, and other Scots lords in an expedition to Palestine. At home he seems to have been entirely overshadowed by his father, as it is not until after the latter's death in 1283 that James takes any leading part in Scottish affairs.

In 1284 he was one of the great Scots Barons who undertook to preserve the succession of the Crown to the grandchild of Alexander III., and two years later, on that Prince's death (1286), he was one of six joint Regents appointed by the Estates of Scotland. Within a few years however the Regency broke up. Of his colleagues, the Earl of Buchan had died, and Duncan Earl of Fife had been murdered by Sir Patrick Abernethy and Sir Walter Percy, at the instigation of Sir William Abernethy; and in 1288, at Turnbery Castle, the Stewart, apparently distrusting the remaining Regents, entered into a Bond of Association with several other Barons with a view to securing, in certain contingencies, the descent of the Crown to his friend Brus. To this Bond the other principal Scots signatories were Robert de Brus, Lord of Annandale, his son Robert de Brus, Earl of Carrick, Patrick Earl of Dunbar and his three sons, cousins of the Stewart, Sir John Stewart of Bonkyl his brother, Walter Stewart Earl of Menteith, his uncle, and that Earl's two sons Sir Alexander and Sir John Menteith.

In 1288 also, the Stewart succeeded Sir Andrew Moray as Sheriff of Ayr, and the following year his accounts are given in by his clerk and factor Reginald, for whose bona-fides Sir John Stewart of Bonkyl appears as surety. His name and that of his uncle, Walter Stewart Earl of Menteith, appear among the magnates present in the Parliament held at Brigham in 1289-90, and in 1292 the same lords, along with Sir John Stewart of Bonkyl, were nominated by Brus to act as three of his representatives or auditors at the trial by Edward I. of the Brus and Baliol claims to the Crown—another instance of the friendship between the House of Brus and that of Stewart.

In common with all the other great Scots lords at that time, the Stewart took an oath of fealty to Edward, and, as one of the governors, gave seisin of the kingdom to Baliol on Edward deciding in favour of the latter's claim.

His complaisance with the existing government, then and afterwards, was however shortlived, and appears to have been dictated wholly by necessity and an entire want of preparation for, or means of, resistance to the power of the ambitious Edward. He took the earliest opportunity to try to shake off the yoke, and in 1297 along with his brother Sir John Stewart of Bonkyl, he joined Wallace, Sir William

I

Douglas, Sir Andrew Moray of Bothwell, and others, in their efforts to free their country. He is said to have also prevailed on Brus to join the struggle.

He was present at the Battle of Stirling in 1297, in which the English were totally defeated by the Scots under Wallace, and along with the Earl of Lennox pursued and harassed the Earl of Surrey in his retreat. The unanimity of the Scottish leaders was however shortlived, and dissensions breaking out regarding precedence and power, the Stewart and Brus, despairing of success under such conditions, again took the oath of allegiance to the prevailing power.

His younger brother Sir John Stewart of Bonkyl however, showed greater strength and determination of character, and continued steady in his opposition to the aggression of England. His action was far from being discouraged by the Stewart, who, though—whether from policy or, according to some accounts, ill-health—taking no active part personally at this time, yet permitted his "Brandanes" or military tenants to take up arms for their country under his brother Sir John Stewart.

The opposing forces found themselves once more arrayed in arms against each other on the field of Falkirk in 1298, and once more the fatal pride of the Scots nobility led to dissension and jealousy, if not absolute treachery. The haughty Comyn, who commanded the Scottish cavalry, led his entire force off the field without striking a blow, and Wallace himself retired in dudgeon with his own force to some distance, leaving Sir John Stewart of Bonkyl and his division to sustain the assault of the whole English army unsupported. The unequal contest was maintained with the utmost gallantry—the long Scottish spears of Sir John Stewart's borderers presenting an impenetrable barrier to the repeated charges of the English cavalry, though their ranks rapidly thinned under the hail of arrows directed against them by the English bowmen. This weapon, unsupported as they were by cavalry, the Scots were altogether unable to contend against, and while encouraging his men to stand fast, their brave leader was himself struck, and falling from his horse, perished in the tumult which ensued. His followers crowded round his body, and, still disdaining to retreat, many perished with him—their gallantry and splendid physical proportions compelling the admiration even of the victorious enemy, whose historians have put on record their praise of the valour and personal appearance of the Scots. Deprived of their leader the Scottish army at length gave way, and retired under cover of night, with the assistance of the force under Wallace, which had remained practically inactive. In addition to Sir John Stewart, Wallace's great friend Sir John Graham, was also slain, and both were interred in the burial-ground at Falkirk. A stone, supposed from its antique configuration to be the original one, still

marks Sir John Stewart's grave, bearing the inscription:
"Here lies a Scottish hero, Sir John Stewart, who was killed
"at the Battle of Falkirk 22 July 1298."

Sir John Stewart married Margaret, the daughter and
heiress of Sir Alexander de Bonkyl in Berwickshire, a family
of rank and possessed of great estates in the border counties
both of Scotland and England. From this circumstance he
is generally designated as "of Bonkyl." As however Sir
Alexander de Bonkyl survived his son-in-law, Sir John Stewart
if he ever actually owned the estate, can only have done so
by resignation of his father-in-law.

By his wife Margaret de Bonkyl, Sir John Stewart left
a family of seven sons and one daughter, Elizabeth, married
to Thomas Randolph, Earl of Moray and Lord of Mar. The
sons were

1. Sir Alexander Stewart, ancestor of the Stewart and
Douglas Earls of Angus.

2. Sir Alan Stewart of Dreghorn, ancestor of the Stuarts,
Dukes and Earls of Lennox, Darnley, D'Aubigny, etc.; the
Stewarts, Earls of Galloway, and other noble houses.

3. Sir Walter Stewart of Dalswinton, also ancestor of the
Earls of Galloway, the Lords Blantyre, etc.

4. Sir James Stewart of Perston and Warwickhill,
ancestor of the Stewart Earls of Buchan, Earls of Athol,
Earls of Traquair, Lords of Lorn, the Stewarts of Appin,
the Stewarts of Grandtully, etc., and their cadets.

5. Sir John Stewart of Daldon,

6. Sir Hugh Stewart, and

7. Sir Robert Stewart, ancestor of the Steuarts of Allanton, Coltness, etc., and their cadets.

This goodly band of knights, inheriting their father's patriotism, afterwards, under Brus, formed part of that bulwark of Scottish independence, in the foundation of which their father sacrificed his life, and in the building up and strengthening of which no fewer than three of them—Sir Alan, Sir James, and Sir John "tres fratres inclites" in the language of Fordun in his "Scotichronicon"—also gave up theirs on the fatal field of Halidon Hill in 1333.

Meantime, in 1302, four years after his brother's death, James, the Stewart of Scotland, once more threw off his allegiance to England, and accompanied by six other ambassadors, set out for France to seek assistance from King Philip to enable his countrymen to continue the war. This step so exasperated Edward that he placed him in the same category as Wallace, and specially exempted him from the benefits of the Act of Indemnity passed in 1304.

Affairs were now, however, rapidly approaching a crisis, and in 1306 the younger Brus, by the slaughter of Sir John (the red) Comyn at Dumfries, gave the signal for a new and ultimately more successful struggle for independence. Brus has been severely censured for this hasty blow by which Comyn lost his life, but consideration of that baron's character and previous history point to the probability that the deed which was to have such momentous consequences to Brus and to Scotland, was perpetrated quite as much in self-defence as in passion or by design.

The Scottish records show that Comyn was a man of fierce and uncontrollable passions, and that the quarrel and assault at Dumfries were not the first or only occurrences of the kind that had taken place between these powerful rivals. Comyn was the principal representative of a family once the most powerful in Scotland, which possessed several earldoms, *e.g.*, Buchan and Menteith, destined not long afterwards to pass into the hands of the Stewarts, and could muster at call over thirty knights of the name. The pride and ambition thus engendered worked their destruction, in which the families of Brus and Stewart had, as has been shown, no small share. Their fall was however too recent to have greatly checked their pride and impatience of all opposition; and a few years previous to his death, Sir John Comyn had (1294) been committed to prison for assaulting the doorkeeper of the Exchequer and breaking his wand of office. Five years later another instance of his ungovernable temper is recorded, where, at a council of the magnates of Scotland, held at Peebles in 1299, "Sir John Comyn leaped "on Robert Brus, Earl of Carrick, and took him by the "throat, and John Comyn, Earl of Buchan, leaped on "William Lamberton, Bishop of St Andrews, and they "held them fast," until "the Stewart and others went "between them and stopped this scuffle." With sidelights such as these thrown on the character of the victim of the tragedy enacted at Dumfries in 1306, no great stretch of imagination is required to conceive that Brus's dagger was unsheathed as much in self-preservation as in passion, and that Comyn fell a victim quite as much to his own fury as to Brus's violence.

For Brus and his friends however, that dagger-stroke was fraught with consequences of the greatest moment to themselves and their descendants.

One of Edward's first acts on learning of Brus's rebellion against English thraldom, was to endeavour to gain possession of Andrew, the eldest son of the Stewart. This youth had, some years previously, been placed by his father in the hands of Edward as a hostage. Edward in turn entrusted him to Lamberton, Bishop of St Andrews, but, knowing the friendship and close association which had for several generations subsisted between the families of Stewart and Brus, no sooner had Brus's act come to his knowledge than he required the Bishop to deliver up the Stewart's heir. Lamberton however, instead of complying placed the youth in the hands of Brus, thereby earning for himself the deadly enmity of Edward. What afterwards became of this hostage is unknown, as his name appears no more in history. His father does not seem at once to have thrown in his lot with Brus, as his name does not appear among those present at his friend's coronation nor among his supporters in his brief and futile attempt in 1306. At what precise time he did join him is uncertain, but it was probably not unconnected with that step that the Monastery of Paisley was burned by the English in 1307. He did not live to see the end of the struggle, dying two years later (July 1309) at the age of sixty-six—one of his last acts being to sign the letter sent by the Scots nobles

in 1309 to Philip of France, in the name of the people of
Scotland, intimating their allegiance to Brus, as King of
Scots. By his wife Cecilia, daughter of Patrick Earl of
Dunbar and March, he left issue surviving him:—Walter,
his successor; Sir John Stewart, killed at the Battle of
Dundalk in 1318 along with Edward Brus Earl of Carrick
and titular King of Ireland; and Sir James Stewart of Durrisdeer, who after his brother Walter's death in 1326, commanded the forces of his nephew, the young Stewart of
Scotland, and accompanied Randolph and Douglas in their
raids into England. James the Stewart also left a daughter,
Egidia or Giles, married to Alexander Menzies, ancestor of
the family of Menzies.

K

Walter, the fourth of that name and sixth hereditary High Stewart, was born in 1293, and thus was only sixteen years old at the time of his father's death. On reaching majority he seems at once to have assumed command of his hereditary retainers, and at the "Muster of Torwood," prior to the Battle of Bannockburn, the young Stewart appeared on the field at the head of a noble body of men to assert the independence of his country and the title of Brus to the throne. Barbour, in his poem "The Bruce," thus describes the Stewart and his forces:—

> "Valtir Stewart of Scotland syne
> "That then wes bot ane berdless hyne
> "Cam with a rout of nobill men
> "That all be contynans micht ken."

Although only twenty-one, the third or centre division of the Scots army was entrusted to him and his cousin Sir James Douglas, a responsibility which his high rank and great feudal power entitled him to, and which the talents for war which he displayed not only at Bannockburn but during the whole of his short though glorious career fully justified. Barbour thus narrates the incident:—

"And syne the thrid battale he gaf
"To Valtir Stewart for to leid
"And till Douglass douchty of deid
"Thai war cosyngis in neir degrie
"Therfor till hym betaucht* wes he.
"For he wes young, but nochtforthi†
"I trow he sall so manlily
"Do his dewoir,‡ and virk so weill
"That hym sall neyd no mair zeymseil." §

The two cousins were knighted by Brus on the field in accordance with the custom of the time. Walter acquitted himself with signal valour and ability, and with Douglas joined in the pursuit of the luckless Edward to the Castle of Berwick. For his services he was appointed Warden of the Western Marches by Brus, who further rewarded him by a grant of Baliol's lands of Largs.

Brus moreover conferred on him perhaps a still more signal mark of his esteem in appointing him his representative to receive on the borders of Scotland and England the persons of many Scots prisoners of high rank, who had long been confined in England, and whose freedom was part of the price which their captors had to pay for the Battle of Bannockburn. Chief among these prisoners were Brus's Queen, his daughter Marjory, and his sister Christian,

---

* Entrusted.　　† Notwithstanding.　　‡ Devoir.　　§ Guardianship.

Countess of Mar. Honours still flowed in on the young Stewart. Having accompanied Brus in 1315 on an expedition for the reduction of the Western Isles, he was, on his return, rewarded with the hand of the King's only daughter, the Princess Marjory, along with whom he received large grants of land in the counties of Edinburgh, Linlithgow, and Stirling. By an Act of the Scots Parliament, Brus secured the succession to the throne to the descendants of Marjory, failing heirs male of his own body or of his brother Edward Brus. The possession of the Scottish throne was thus opened to the Stewarts, but Brus's intentions were well-nigh frustrated by the sudden death of his daughter in less than a year after her marriage. On Shrove Tuesday 1316, when returning from Paisley Abbey to the Castle of Renfrew, she was thrown from her horse and so seriously injured that she died in a few hours, after giving birth to a son subsequently known in history as Robert II., King of Scots. The Princess was interred in Paisley Abbey, the last resting-place of so many of her husband's ancestors and friends, and in the devotional spirit of the age, the lands of Largs, which he had so recently received as a reward of his valour, were gifted by the Stewart to the Abbey, for prayers for the safety of the souls of Marjory Brus and himself.

Meantime the fiery Edward Brus, tiring of the peace which ensued in Scotland after the Battle of Bannockburn, had accepted the invitation of some of the Irish chiefs, and sailed for the neighbouring island to assume the Crown of Ireland, and to carry on there against the English that warfare which was denied him at home, and which the memory of his slaughtered brothers and friends seemed ever to call for at his hands. In his train went many of the best and noblest knights of Scotland, including several of the Stewart's near relatives. After carrying on the war in Ulster with varying success for about two years, disaster at length overtook King Edward. He was opposed by a strong English force at Dundalk in 1318, and, contrary to the advice of his knights insisted on fighting. Sir John Stewart, younger brother of the High Stewart of Scotland, and who had already been severely wounded by a spear-thrust earlier in the war, in vain besought him to await the arrival of reinforcements which were coming up, but the headstrong Brus, rejecting all counsel, ordered his troops to engage. In the battle which ensued, King Edward paid the penalty of his rashness with his life, and by his side fell Sir John Stewart and many more of the Scottish chivalry. Numerous prisoners were taken by the English, including Sir Alan Stewart, eldest son of Sir John Stewart of Darnley and Crookston, and cousin of the unfortunate Sir John who lost his life on the same field.

Early in the war, King Robert of Scotland himself had passed over to Ireland to his brother's assistance, leaving as Regents during his absence, his son-in-law Walter the Stewart, and Sir James Douglas.

War with England having once more broken out, siege was laid to the great border fortress of Berwick, which at length fell into the hands of the Scots. The charge of this important stronghold was committed by Bruce to the Stewart, who, knowing that the most strenuous efforts would be made by the English for its recovery, made corresponding preparations for its defence. Five hundred gentlemen and their retainers who quartered the arms of the Stewart by right of birth or feudal dependence, repaired to his standard to form part of the garrison and share in the glory of the coming struggle.

While the expected attack was being awaited, the Stewart was temporarily summoned to Scone to witness a new Act of Parliament, passed on 3rd December 1318, by which, failing heirs male of the body of King Robert himself, the Stewart's infant son Robert was declared heir to the Scottish Crown in right of his mother Marjory Brus. By this later Statute, the heirs of Edward Brus were excluded, and the succession vested in the descendants of Robert Brus alone.

A few months after Walter's return from this ceremony, the anticipated siege of Berwick by the English was begun. In the autumn of 1319 Edward II. in person led a great army

into Scotland and assaulted Berwick both by sea and land
On 7th September 1319, ships sailed close under the walls,
and endeavoured to drop bridges from their masts by means
of which the soldiery on board might obtain access to the
walls, which at that time were so low that an enemy on
foot could, with a spear, reach the defenders on the top.
Simultaneously with the naval attack an assault was also
delivered by land, but inspired by the presence and example
of their young leader the garrison successfully repelled both.
The naval attempt in particular failed ignominiously, and one
of the ships having grounded was left by the receding tide
at the mercy of the Scots, who promptly set it on fire and
burned it to the water's edge.

Six days afterwards, 13th September 1319, a second and
still more determined assault was delivered. Ships, fitted u
for the reception of archers in the tops and rigging, and wit
bridges for dropping on the ramparts, sailed up the river.
huge machine, called a "sow," and movable scaffolds,
constructed to contain and protect the attacking force in
advance, were dragged up to the walls under cover of ga
showers of arrows from the shipping in the river. T
machines the Scots, however, managed to overthrow or des
and the huge "sow" itself was at length wrecked by a
hurled from a catapult by John Crab, a Flemish engin
the garrison. Falling directly on the top of the "sow
mass crashed through the roof of boards and hides, cr

in its course the unfortunate soldiers who occupied the machine. The wreck was immediately grappled by the Scots, and having been hauled close under the wall, pitch, flax, and other combustibles were thrown on it, and the whole set on fire. The springalds and catapults on the ramparts also disconcerted and defeated the efforts of the enemy from the water, but the main, or land attack was pressed by King Edward II. with all his available force, and maintained from early morning until darkness set in. The Stewart, attended by a select body of a hundred personal friends, patrolled the walls throughout the whole day, detaching members of his bodyguard where the exigencies of the siege demanded extra support or fresh leadership. In spite of all the efforts of the garrison however, the English at length by force of numbers succeeded in filling up the ditch and fixing their ladders to the wall, but more they were unable to accomplish. In the afternoon they captured the drawbridge and set fire to the gate at St Mary's Port. The Stewart immediately hastened thither attended by the only member of his hundred personal followers then left him. Perceiving the serious nature of the situation he determined on the desperate expedient of a sally, and calling down the guard from the rampart, he ordered the gate to be thrown open, and rushing through the flames of the burning port fiercely attacked the enemy in his turn. The terrible combat which followed was heroically maintained by the Scots on most unequal terms until nightfall, when the English com-

manders, foiled on every hand and utterly disheartened, with-drew their troops from the assault.

Although thus twice defeated, the importance of Berwick would doubtless have led Edward to make a third attempt to recapture it from the Scots. Brus however created a diversion in favour of his gallant son-in-law and his brave garrison, by sending the renowned Randolph and Douglas at the head of 15,000 men to raid the north of England. Thus, while his country's whole military power lay baffled and defeated before Berwick, Edward received intelligence that the dreaded Douglas and Randolph had suddenly broken into England, and being opposed by the Church vassals and ecclesiastics had easily defeated these troops in a battle, called with the grim irony of the time, "the Chapter of "Mitton," from the numerous priests and other churchmen who fell in the fight. The English loss in killed alone was upwards of 4000; and many of his barons, especially those whose estates lay exposed to the Scottish raiders, having deserted him on receipt of these news, Edward had no alternative but to abandon the siege. Chalmers in his "Cale-"donia" says: "The defence of Berwick by so young a soldier, "displays a talent and valour of which a nation may boast."

The restless Douglas continued to harass the borders of England long after the original object of his expedition—the diversion of the attacks on Berwick—had been accomplished, burning and ravaging Cumberland and Westmoreland, destroy-

L

ing the stores of grain, and driving numerous herds of sheep and cattle a prey into Scotland.

In the following year, 1320, the Scots barons sent their famous letter and remonstrance to the Pope, in which they declared the independence of their country and the right of Brus to the throne. To that letter the Stewart was one of the principal signatories.

In 1321, Walter received a grant of the baronies of Nisbet and Eckford and other lands, in Roxburghshire, formerly owned by Sir William de Soulis and Sir Roger de Mowbray, and forfeited by reason of the adherence of these knights to the English interest.

Edward having succeeded in restoring a certain amount of harmony between his barons and himself, in 1322 again led a large force into Scotland, but was once more compelled ignominiously to retreat, the Scots having, according to the usual tactics of Brus, retired before him wasting their own country as they went and thus leaving nothing for the support and maintenance of an enemy. For this compulsory sacrifice however, Brus exacted the customary penalty. No sooner had the baffled Edward recrossed the border than Brus and his three great captains—Douglas, Randolph, and the Stewart—burst into England in their turn. Brus and the Stewart invested Norham Castle, while Douglas and Randolph pursued the old harassing and desultory warfare. The four leaders having united their forces, at length met and entirely defeated the English army at Beland Abbey in Yorkshire; and so complete was the overthrow that Edward himself barely escaped with his life, being chased off the field by the Stewart at the head of 500 horse, and pursued to the very gates of York. Barbour narrates that in the chivalrous spirit of the age, the Stewart, to give Edward a chance of retrieving his honour, waited at the gates till evening, "to see if any would "ish and fight." But his challenge was not accepted, and at nightfall he led his little band back to his compatriots. In his haste to escape from his fiery pursuer on this occasion, the luckless Edward repeated his experiences after Bannockburn, and for the second time in his inglorious reign lost the Privy Seal of England.

After this decisive victory, the Scots, with fire and sword laid waste the whole of England north of the Humber, levied enormous sums of ransom and redemption money from the wealthier towns and monasteries, and at length returned into Scotland sweeping before them great herds of cattle, and a multitude of prisoners both of high and low degree. A shortlived truce resulted, of which, on behalf of Scotland, the Stewart was one of the guarantors. This is practically his last public appearance of any importance. He died three years later, 9th April 1326, at his moated Castle of Bathgate, at the early age of thirty-three, to the great grief not only of the King and his other friends and companions in arms, but of the whole people of Scotland, by whom he seems to have been deeply and deservedly respected. When a mere youth he had done good service for his country at Bannockburn, and his sword had practically never been laid aside during his whole after life. "Had he lived," says Lord Hailes, "he might have equalled "Randolph and Douglas, but his course of glory was short."

Walter the Stewart, was thrice married: 1st, to Alice, daughter of Sir John Erskine of Erskine, of which marriage there was one daughter, Jean, married to Hugh, Earl of Ross; 2nd, to the Princess Marjory Brus, who, as has been indicated, survived her marriage less than a year, leaving an only son, afterwards King Robert II.; and 3rd, to Isabel, sister of Sir John Graham of Abercôrn, by whom he had two sons, Sir John Stewart and Sir Andrew Stewart, and a daughter, Lady Egidia Stewart. This branch of the Stewarts is, throughout, designed of "Railstoun," whether actually in possession of the lands or not.

Egidia was thrice married, and died in 1396, leaving children by her first and second husbands at least.

By Sir James Lindsay of Crawford (who seems to have died about 1358) she had one son, also Sir James Lindsay of Crawford, who married the heiress of Fremartine, Margaret, daughter of Sir William Keith, Marischal of Scotland. This second Sir James Lindsay was for a time Sheriff of Perth, but fell into disgrace in 1382 through murdering the King's son-in-law, Sir James Lyon (Chamberlain of Scotland), and he himself died in 1397, leaving two daughters, married respectively to Sir Thomas Colville and Sir John Herries of Terreagles.

By Sir James Lindsay her first husband, Lady Egidia Stewart also left a daughter, Isabel Lindsay, who married Sir John Maxwell of Pollok.

The Lady Egidia's second husband was Sir Hugh of Eglinton, who died in 1376, leaving issue a daughter, Elizabeth, who married John Montgomery of Eaglesham, and thus was ancestress of the Earls of Eglinton.

Her third husband was Sir James Douglas of Dalkeith.

Of Sir Andrew Stewart of Railstoun not much is known. He enjoyed an annuity from the Customs of Perth and Dundee, appears in receipt of various gifts of money from the King, and must have died in or about 1413, as in the Accounts then audited he is described as "quondam."

The most important of the Railstoun line was the eldest son, Sir John Stewart, who appears to have received from his father Walter the Stewart, a grant of the lands of Railstoun in Cunningham, which, as has been said, appear to have given a title not only to himself and sons but to his brother. These lands are not to be mistaken for those of Ralstoun near Paisley, owned by the Ralstouns of that ilk.

In 1357-8 Sir John Stewart of Railstoun had a royal grant of the "fermes" of Rate, and from 1370 to 1378 was Steward of the household to his brother King Robert II., his salary in that capacity being £20! From 1380 till his death in 1416, at the great age of ninety-two, he appears in receipt of an annuity of £20, paid either by the Chamberlain or by the

Custumars of Perth. He has been—apparently erroneously—identified with the John Stewart who was of David II.'s household at the Château Gaillard in France, and there contracted a marriage with Alice, the daughter of the Royal Chamberlain, Sir Reginald More. This however seems contradicted by the fact that if grown up at that time—1334-1340—he must have been over 100 years of age at the time of his death in 1416—his father, Walter the Stewart of Scotland, having died in 1426, at which time if Sir John was of marriageable age in 1334-40, he must have been nine or ten years old since he had at least one brother younger than himself, namely, Sir Andrew referred to above. He left two sons, Sir Walter and Sir John (and perhaps a third Robert), and three daughters, Marjory, Egidia, and Margaret.

Of Sir John Stewart, the second son, little is known. He appears in an Exchequer Roll of 1382 as " brother of the lord " Walter Stewart," and again in one of 1386 as " nephew of " the King."

Sir Walter Stewart of Railstoun played a very prominent part in Scotland, England, and France.

As " Lord Walter Stewart," he received a gift from the King in 1379, and in 1380 was employed by David, Earl of Strathern, who paid him that year a salary of £10.

He appears as Sir Walter Stewart of Railstoun in 1391 and 1394, and though his father was certainly still alive, he must either have been in possession of, or had some interest in, the lands prior to his father's death, as in 1396 he pledged them to Hugh Wallace of Craigie for a debt of 200 marks. He was Sheriff of Perth from 1381 to 1385 at least, and along with his cousin and namesake, Walter Stewart Earl of Athole (son of King Robert II.), he was engaged in attempting the pacification of the Highlands, and was also much occupied in missions to England, France, and Rome. Soon after the death of his uncle King Robert II., he was deputed to proceed to Paris to renew the ancient league with France, and £40 was paid for his "expenses on the King's business in distant "parts" in 1391. He was also entrusted by his cousin—the Duke of Albany—with an embassy to England to negotiate the release of Sir Murdoch Stewart the Duke's eldest son. Having no nearer heirs, he conveyed his lands of Railstoun (soon after his father's death in 1416) to his nephew William Douglas of Lugton, the son of his sister Marjory and Sir William Douglas of Lugton and Lochleven. He appears to have died about 1438, and with him the direct line of the Stewarts of Railstoun became extinct.

In the "Chronicles of Pluscarden," already quoted and apparently written by a contemporaneous historian, a Robert Stewart of Railstoun is mentioned as one of the heroes of the Battle of Beaugé in 1421. The Chronicle narrates that out of respect for Passion Week a truce had been agreed upon between the English—commanded by the Duke of Clarence, brother of Henry V. of England—and the French and the Scots auxiliaries commanded by John Stewart Earl of Buchan, and Sir John Stewart of Darnley. The English however treacherously broke the truce, and endeavoured to surprise their enemies, who were unsuspectingly enjoying themselves. Fortunately however a small outlying body of Scots under Robert Stewart of Railstoun, Hugh Kennedy, and John Smayle of Aberdeen, were stationed by the side of a river which the English had to cross, and observed through the trees the banners of the approaching foe. The leaders of the Scots at once sent messengers to warn their comrades, and disposed their little force to dispute the passage of the stream in order to give their main body time to arm and reach the scene of action. In their anxiety to take the enemy by surprise, the English had left their archers and infantry behind, trusting to their heavily-armed knights and cavalry to ride down opposition. But, says the quaint old Chronicle, "the Scots are most mighty " men at a sudden charge, and very good with the spear," and Stewart and his comrades made good the national reputation. The gallant defenders were slowly but surely reinforced, and, assuming the offensive, bore down the leading ranks of the enemy. The main body of the French and Scots coming up, the battle became general and raged till nightfall, ending in the utter defeat of the English, who lost 1500 men in killed alone, including their leader and twenty-six other lords and knights, while the Earls of Somerset, Dorset, and Huntingdon and many other nobles were taken prisoners. The Duke of Clarence was killed by one of the Earl of Buchan's household, and his coronet was purchased after the battle by Sir John Stewart of Darnley for 1000 crowns.

The "Chronicle of Pluscarden" goes on to relate that after this defeat, Henry V. returned from England to prosecute the war in person, but was overtaken by a grievous sickness which the doctors pronounced incurable, and which the priests ascribed to St Fiacre in retribution for the desecration of his relics by the English soldiery. Making enquiry as to the saint who was thus punishing him, the English monarch learned that St Fiacre was the son of a Scottish King, upon which Henry is reported to have said: "This is a cursed nation " wherever I go I find them under my nose. No wonder " they are savage and revengeful in life when" (alluding to the saint) " they work such cruel vengeance after death."

This " Robert Stewart of Railstoun " appears in no other records, and it has therefore been thought not improbable that the Christian name has been wrongly transcribed in the Chronicle, and that the hero of Beaugé was really Sir Walter Stewart of Railstoun, who undoubtedly was several times in France in various capacities.

Marjory Stewart, the eldest sister of Sir Walter Stewart of Railstoun, became the second wife of Sir Alexander Lindsay of Glenesk, who died in 1382, and by whom she had two sons, Sir William Lindsay of Rossie and Sir Walter Lindsay. Between 1382 and 1387 she married Sir Henry

M

Douglas of Lugton and Lochleven (who seems to have died between 1392 and 1393) and her son by this marriage—Sir William Douglas, afterwards of Lochleven—succeeded his uncle Sir Walter Stewart, in the lands of Railstoun as already indicated. She appears in the accounts of the time (under various designations, "Marjory Lindsay," "wife of Sir Henry "Douglas," "niece of the King," "widow of Sir Henry "Douglas") in the receipt of various pensions and annuities, which like most others of the class, disappear under the stern auditing of King James the First. She seems to have died about 1439.

Her sister Egidia Stewart was the second wife of Sir Patrick Graham of Kincardine and Dundaff, whom she seems to have married about 1384. The son of this marriage, Sir Patrick Graham, married Euphemia Stewart, Countess Palatine of Strathern and Countess of Caithness—the only child of King Robert II.'s son David, Earl of Strathern and Caithness. On her marriage the Countess of Strathern received a gift of £116, 13s. 4d. from the King. Her son, Malise Graham, was deprived by King James the First, of the Earldom of Strathern, on the plea that it was a male fief—an injudicious and even unjust act, which not indirectly cost the Sovereign his life.

Margaret Stewart, the third daughter of Sir John Stewart of Railstoun, married in 1388 Sir John Hay, with a dowry of 100 marks from her uncle King Robert II. Sir John was the lord of Boyne and Enzie in Banff, and of

Touch and Tullibody in Clackmannan. Her daughter and heir became the second wife of Alexander, Earl of Huntly, and ancestress of the Setons of Touch.

It was in the time of Walter, the sixth hereditary High Stewart of Scotland, that the Stewart lands were augmented by the extensive territory of Kilbride as well as those others already mentioned in the history of his life. He was buried with his fathers in the Abbey of Paisley, to which, like them, he had been a liberal benefactor.

In the Charter Chest of the Earl of Strathmore, a charter by this Walter still exists, with his seal attached. The seal displays, on obverse, an armed knight riding towards the sinister, his helmet surmounted by a framework carrying a lion rampant, facing to sinister, and his shield bearing the Stewart "fesse," which is repeated on the housings, and also on the collar, of the horse. The reverse bears simply a shield charged with the "Fesse chequé," and surrounded by figures of leopards. The legends are indistinct,

"WALTE . . . . . E" and "S . . . . . SCOCIE."

Walter was succeeded by his son Robert, destined to play a more important part, and to experience greater vicissitudes of fortune than any of his predecessors. At his father's death he was only ten years of age, and three years later his grandfather, King Robert de Brus, after whom he was named, also died, leaving as heirs to the Crown of Scotland and its troubles, two boys—his son David Brus, aged six, and his grandson Robert Stewart, aged thirteen.

An entry appears in the Exchequer Rolls of 1329 for the expense of cloth for the robes of " the Senescal " at King Robert's funeral, but whether the word is intended to relate to Robert the Stewart of Scotland, or simply to the steward of the King's household, is not clear.

In terms of the Act of Settlement of 1318, Thomas Randolph Earl of Moray, the nephew of the late King, assumed the Regency during the minority of the heir. In addition to being the greatest military leader then left to Scotland — his old comrades and rivals in renown, Brus, Douglas, and Walter the Stewart, having all predeceased him—he was nearly related to both heirs. By birth he was a full cousin of the young King, David II., his mother being

Isabel Brus, a sister of King Robert, while through his wife Isabel Stewart, only daughter of Sir John Stewart of Bonkyl, and full cousin of Walter the Stewart, he was by marriage second cousin to the young Stewart of Scotland, the next heir to the throne. Indeed, it is noteworthy that the four great Scottish leaders, Brus, Douglas, Randolph, and Stewart, who achieved their country's independence, and asserted it so heroically while life remained, were united not only in the closest friendship, but by the still dearer ties of blood and marriage.

As further showing this intimate relationship and also the hazards of war, it may be interesting to state that the celebrated Douglas, in the raids through the South of Scotland with which he so harassed and annoyed the English during the early part of the War of Independence, captured his cousin, Sir Alexander Stewart of Bonkyl, and Brus's nephew, Thomas Randolph, in hiding in a house of Randolph's on Lyne Water in Peeblesshire. These barons had not then declared for Brus, but on being brought to the King by Douglas they at once espoused his cause and maintained it ever afterwards with the utmost gallantry and fidelity. Randolph's famous career from that time onwards is well known, but that of his friend and brother-in-law Sir Alexander Stewart of Bonkyl — whose only sister (Isabel) Randolph married—is less known. He appears to have died young, but his services were rewarded by Brus with the Earldom of Angus, which Earldom it is also curious to observe came in later years, through the heiress of the Stewart Earls of Angus, to a representative of his captor, Sir James Douglas.

While Randolph lived, the government of Scotland was successfully carried on, the terror of his name and the remembrance of the exploits of this leader, only less dreaded in his day than Douglas, securing also peace and freedom from invasion.

Prompted however by the barons, both English and Scottish, whose estates in Scotland had been forfeited by Brus, Edward III. at length threatened war. Randolph at once prepared for the encounter, but after having assembled and set his troops in motion to meet the invaders, he was overtaken by disease and died on the march on the 26th July 1332.

An unhappy choice of a successor was made in the person of Donald Earl of Mar, another cousin of the King, and son of Christian Brus, sister of the late King Robert, but a man altogether deficient in the qualities which ensured the success of his predecessor's government. His regency was however of short duration, as in less than a month he was surprised, defeated, and slain, at the disgraceful rout of Dupplin Moor, near Perth, on 12th August 1332—a battle in which many of the Scots nobility perished, including Robert Brus, Earl of Carrick, a natural son of King Robert Brus, Thomas

Randolph Earl of Moray, the son and heir of the great Randolph, and Murdoch Stewart Earl of Menteith. The losses at this battle were indeed so great and the blow to the Scots so severe, that, in less than three months, Baliol, the son of Brus's old rival, found himself in quiet possession of Scotland, the Crown of which he assumed at Scone on 24th September 1332.

The spirits of the Scots soon revived however, and after conferring the dangerous office of Regent on Sir Andrew Moray of Bothwell, brother-in-law of the late and uncle of the present King, they began once more to harry the English borders. The principal stronghold of the English faction at this time was Galloway, of whose ancient lords Baliol was the direct representative, and for whom, as the grandson of Devorgoile—one of the three co-heiresses whose rights were championed so stoutly by Alexander the Stewart in the time of Alexander II. — both the nobility and commons of the district entertained a warm affection. While lying in fancied security at Annan, Baliol was suddenly attacked by the adherents of David Brus, led by Sir Archibald Douglas, youngest brother of the "Good Lord James," accompanied by Sir Simon Fraser and John Randolph, second son of the great Randolph, and Earl of Moray since his elder brother's death at Dupplin. These leaders, assembling a body of horsemen in Annandale, fell on Baliol's camp in the darkness, slew his brother Henry and many of his principal followers, and chased the new crowned King from the country. Baliol, almost naked and with hardly an attendant, escaped into England, from which however, reinforced by his friends there, he returned in the following March (1333) and laid siege to Berwick. The Regent, Sir Andrew Moray, hastened to its relief, but falling into the hands of the English by the way, was conducted to Edward III. at Durham and confined in close custody. Almost simultaneously with the loss of the Regent, Scotland lost another of her most capable leaders through the capture of Sir William Douglas, the Black Knight of Liddesdale, at Lochmaben.

In these circumstances the Regency was next entrusted to Sir Archibald Douglas, already mentioned, who by way of retaliation led an army into Northumberland. Receiving however representations as to the straits in which the garrison of Berwick was placed, he decided to abandon his raid and march to the relief of the beleaguered town. He was met by the English at Halidon Hill, and there, failing to profit by the lessons and examples of his great brother and his compeers in regard to the dreaded clothyard arrow of the English archers, was completely routed within sight of the town he had come to relieve (13th July 1333).

To that disastrous fight the young Stewart of Scotland, then about sixteen years of age, brought a numerous body of men, and under his uncle Sir James Stewart of Durrisdeer and Rossyth, fought throughout the day at the head of the second division of the Scottish army. Among the killed were the Regent himself and many of the chief nobility of Scotland. The young Stewart and his uncle, Sir James of Rossyth (himself severely wounded) at the close of the fight succeeded in extricating a part of his forces, but his cousins Sir Alan Stewart of Darnley, Sir James Stewart of Perston, and Sir John Stewart of Daldon—sons of Sir John Stewart of Bonkyl, and ancestors of the Stewarts of Darnley and D'Aubigny, Lennox, Galloway, Buchan, Traquair, Atholl, Appin, etc.—lay slain on the field.

Lord Hailes also includes in his list of the killed, a Sir Walter Stewart who fought in the division commanded by Randolph Earl of Moray, but who cannot be identified.

So heavy were the losses of the Scots in the fatal Battle of Halidon Hill that it was generally thought in England that the Scottish wars were ended, since no man seemed left to the unfortunate country, possessed either of sufficient rank or importance to muster an army, or of skill to lead one in the field.

The jubilation of Baliol and his friends was however short-lived. Sir Malcolm Fleming of Cumbernauld had escaped the slaughter at Halidon, and secured the Castle of Dumbarton and the person of the young King. With him also the young Stewart took refuge for a time till he could pass into his ancestral territory of Bute. There, a fugitive, he lay concealed for some months, while Baliol proclaimed him a rebel, confiscated his vast estates, which he bestowed on David de Strathbogie Earl of Athole, and conferred his hereditary office of Stewart of Scotland on the ambitious Edward of England, who had purchased the self-asserted rights of the Earl of Arundel to the office.

Robert however did not remain long in idleness, but with a prudence and determination beyond his years, organised a course of action. With the assistance of two old servants he crossed to the mainland, and aided by his relative, Sir Dugald Campbell of Lochaw, he attacked and captured the Castle of Dunoon. His adherents in Bute learning of this early success of his arms, rose in his service, attacked and slew Alan de Lisle the governor, and presented his head to their master. Following up the attack, they captured the governor of the Castle of Rothesay, who surrendered his charge to the Stewart. Thus encouraged, he carried the war into Ayrshire, where he received the submission of the English governor, Godfrey de Ros, and proceeding thence into Renfrewshire, recovered his paternal estates in that shire, and by military execution compelled the inhabitants to return to their allegiance to his uncle David II.

The young Stewart at this time is described by Fordun as a "comely youth, tall and robust, modest, liberal, gay and "courteous, and, for the innate sweetness of his disposition, "generally beloved by all true-hearted Scotsmen."

Numerous patriots who had lain concealed in Annandale now flocked to his standard. John Randolph Earl of Moray, the men of Kyle under Thomas Brus (a natural son of King Edward Brus, and ancestor of the Bruses of Clackmannan, where for his services he afterwards received large estates), William de Carruthers and other principal barons joined forces with him, and, strengthened by these accessions, the Stewart speedily reduced Clydesdale, compelled the English governor of Ayr to acknowledge David, and swept the adherents of Baliol and Edward from Renfrew, Carrick, and Cunningham.

The following account of the Stewart and his actions at this time, as narrated by the chronicler of Pluscarden, is of considerable interest and importance, as that history was written in the time of the Stewart's grandson King James I. of Scotland, when the deeds and the actors of so comparatively recent a time were still fresh in the hearts and minds of the people.

"Now when the natives of the country heard that their
"lord, Robert Stewart, had thus entered the country, there
"flocked to him some fellow countrymen of his from Bute, a
"people called the Brandans, who came to his assistance of
"their own accord. They were however cut off by Alan Lile,
"the Sheriff of the country, who hemmed them in on all sides
"in a narrow pass, and, unarmed as they were, endeavoured to
"kill them without mercy. But these Brandans seeing them-
"selves thus unarmed and surrounded by armed men on every
"side, and seeing there was nothing for it but to defend
"themselves manfully, posted themselves in a stony place and
"defended themselves by throwing stones with their hands;
"and there they slew the aforesaid Sheriff and many of the
"nobles of his army by showering stones upon them like hail,
"and forced the rest of his army to turn and flee in haste.
"Then they came to their lord and presented to him the head
"of the said Sheriff, and with the spoils of the slain they armed
"their comrades; but they asked of their lord nothing else as
"their reward, but to become freed for ever from the slavish
"service and duty of multure. This was gladly granted them,
"and they still enjoy this privilege. In this fight with stones,
"John Gibson, the captain of Bute, was taken, and straightway
"surrendered to him the Castle of Bute, and did him homage
"as his natural lord. But as it became noised abroad that
"fortune was smiling upon him, one of his partisans of the
"name of William Carruthers, who had long been hiding in

" concealment in Annandale, and had never allowed himself to
" be won over to the allegiance of the King of England, on
" learning this gathered his friends and partisans together and
" betook himself to the said Robert Stewart, who welcomed
" them gladly and was rejoiced beyond measure. In like
" manner also Thomas Brus joined him with his best men,
" natives of Kyle. Thus his friends and well-wishers came to
" him daily from all parts, and his army waxed stronger day
" by day at their own expense. But the youth, developing in
" age and character and virtue and strength, became comely
" in appearance beyond the children of men. He was large
" and tall in stature, very merry and amiable, affable to all,
" kind and modest and honourable and bountiful, and nature
" endowed him with so much inborn grace that he was
" cordially beloved by all his lieges."

Making liberal allowance for the florid language of the
old chronicler, it is still plain that the personal charm and
fascination of manner which the ill-fated Royal line of the
Stewarts admittedly possessed for all who came into frequent
and intimate intercourse with them, had been hereditary in
their family for many a generation.

Although only about eighteen or nineteen years of age, the
great talents for war thus early displayed, proving the young
Stewart to be the worthy offspring and representative of his
warlike father Walter, and equally so of his renowned grandfather the Brus himself, led the Scottish barons to confer on

him the office of Regent jointly with the brave young Sir John Randolph, Earl of Moray. The first expedition of the new Regents was directed against Baliol's creature, David de Strathbogie Earl of Athole, who now lorded it over a considerable part of the hereditary estates of the Stewart. By a rapid march Randolph surprised Athole, drove him into the wilds of Lochaber, and compelled him to surrender. About this time however some dispute, or at least difference of opinion, appears to have occurred between the Regents, as in the Exchequer Rolls of 1337 the Stewart is said to have collected all the revenues by his own men—instead of by the usual officers—and to have personally uplifted the Burgh Customs of Aberdeen. Whatever the nature or cause of the dispute, it was ended by the capture of the Earl of Moray by the English, upon which fresh misfortune his office of Regent was conferred on Sir Andrew Moray of Bothwell, by whom the office had been previously held up till the time of his capture. In 1338 Sir Andrew Moray died, and the Stewart, who had now attained his majority, was thereafter appointed sole Regent.

Immediately on assuming the Regency, the Stewart made vigorous preparations for expelling Baliol and the English from Scotland. In 1339 he appeared before Perth, the seat of Baliol's government, which, after a gallant resistance extending over four months, was surrendered by Ughtred, the English governor, who with his troops was conducted out of Scotland by the orders of the Stewart. The Castle of Stirling was the Regent's next object, and this stronghold also fell into his hands on the same conditions as Perth. Continuing his march he dislodged the English from all their posts in the north, and afterwards made a progress through Scotland, administering justice, redressing grievances, and restoring good order. The south country fortresses, Edinburgh, Roxburgh, Lochmaben, Berwick, and Jedburgh, still remained in the hands of the enemy, along with the country adjacent, but in 1341 the Castle of Edinburgh was surprised and the garrison overpowered and expelled.

A few months later, King David, who had been sent to France for safety in 1334, after the Battle of Halidon Hill, returned to his native country, and, though only seventeen, assumed the reins of government, which his nephew the Stewart at once resigned into his hands. The latter's conduct as Regent is thus summed up in the "Chronicles of "Pluscarden" already quoted :—

"Though a young man, he bore himself like an old man "against the English nation, and ruled the kingdom most "vigorously and nobly until King David's arrival from "France."

The Stewart accompanied his uncle in the invasion of England which the King undertook shortly after his return, and again in the ill-fated expedition four years later which resulted in the disastrous Battle of Durham, 17th October 1346.

The right wing of the Scots army that day was commanded by John Randolph Earl of Moray, and Sir William Douglas the Knight of Liddesdale. The King in person commanded the centre, while the left was under the leadership of the Stewart and the Earl of March. The gallant Randolph perished early in the fight, and his colleague Douglas was captured. Deprived of their leaders, the right wing gave way, weakening and exposing the centre, where King David, sustaining his share in the conflict with a valour worthy of the son of Brus, was at length severely wounded and made prisoner. The left wing fared better. Being galled by the English archers, the Stewart rushed on them at the head of his troops with such fury as to drive them back on Percy's division. This new force he next fiercely assailed with axe and broadsword, and at length succeeded in throwing them into complete disorder. At this juncture however, Baliol timeously came to Percy's relief with a numerous body of fresh cavalry, and overpowered by numbers and exhausted by their exertions the Stewart's troops were at length compelled to retreat. This movement their leader however conducted with such skill as to discourage Baliol from attempting to harass or attack him, and he at length succeeded in withdrawing his force with a loss, inconsiderable indeed in relation to that of the rest of the army, but including his cousins Sir John Stewart of Darnley and his brother Sir Alan Stewart, together with another unidentified Sir John Stewart amongst the killed, and a third cousin Sir John Stewart of Dalswinton, a Sir Alexander Stewart, another Sir John Stewart and the husband of Margaret Stewart, Countess of Menteith, prisoners in the hands of the enemy.

It has been objected against the Stewart on this occasion that it was his duty at all hazards to have returned to the fight and attempted the rescue of the King. It is however more than probable that such a course was impossible at the stage of the battle at which he succeeded in extricating and withdrawing his troops. The courage and generalship which he then and always displayed is the best answer to such criticism, while the losses amongst his own immediate relatives, who no doubt would fight under the banner of their chief, is proof of the severity of the conflict in which the left wing had been engaged.

Whether the rescue of the King was possible or not, fortunate in any case it was for Scotland that the Stewart acted as he did, since the shattered remnants of the army which he was able to withdraw from the field—for the loss of which the King's obstinate disregard of all advice must be held mainly responsible—were the only forces left to maintain the independence of his country, which once more practically lay at the mercy of the victors.

In this fresh calamity the Stewart was again elected Regent, figuring in the records of the time as Robert, Stewart of Scotland, Lieutenant ("locum tenens") of the most serene Prince David, illustrious King of Scots. He at once entered into negotiations for his unfortunate uncle's release, and sent money to England for his maintenance. For many years he laboured unweariedly for the freedom of King David, but the ransom demanded from a country so impoverished by long and bloody wars was utterly beyond the resources of Scotland.

In the meantime the internal affairs of the country were not neglected, and in the words of Lord Hailes, " notwithstanding " the national calamities the Stewart supported the cause of " his absent sovereign, and maintained a show of civil govern- " ment in Scotland." He made a progress into Galloway, and compelled M'Dowall of Galloway, the turbulent supporter of Baliol, to swear fealty to David at Cumnock in 1353. The following year, in his efforts to obtain his sovereign's freedom, he bound himself to give one of his sons as a perpetual hostage to Edward, beginning with the eldest and so on in succession, till David's ransom should be paid. The negotiations however proving fruitless, the struggle was renewed. Baliol indeed, weary of the constant and futile strife, and of a sovereignty which he possessed only in name, in 1355 resigned in favour of the ambitious King of England, not only his pretensions to the throne, but to various private estates in Scotland, and retired to his French possessions. That year also the Stewart's relative, Thomas Stewart Earl of Angus, grandson of Sir John Stewart of Bonkyl, collected ships, and, as the chronicler of Pluscarden has it, "with a mighty arm and with a strong hand, went by " sea at night" to Berwick, and scaled the walls next the sea. Simultaneously, Dunbar, Earl of March, assisted by a body of French auxiliaries whom he had brought over some months previously, attacked on the land side, and by their combined efforts the town was captured. The Stewart thereupon proceeded to Berwick, made provision for its support, and thanked and dismissed the auxiliaries. The reasons for this last step were doubtless the cost of maintaining these foreign troops, unaccustomed to the hardy methods of living in Scotland, and also the risk of quarrels between two forces so different in every respect, but Lord Hailes also thinks that the Stewart's distrust of the Earl of March, on account of that lord's previous league with England and his constant opposition to the Regent's efforts for a truce or the release of the King, was not unconnected with the dismissal of the French auxiliaries whom the Earl had introduced.

In 1356, Edward III. led a numerous army into Scotland, and burned the Counties of Haddington and Edinburgh. The

Stewart however, mindful of the advice of his illustrious grandfather King Robert,* gave orders for the people to retire before
the enemy, denuding the country as they went of all means of
support.   King Edward was thereby compelled through want
of food to retrace his steps, his own previous severities
during his march northwards now bringing heavy retribution
on himself.   In his retreat he was pursued and harassed by the
Regent's eldest son, John Stewart, Lord of Kyle and Earl of
Carrick,—afterwards known in history as Robert III.,—who,
carrying his arms into Nithsdale, compelled that district to
submit to David.

The following year the Stewart's efforts for his uncle's
release were at length crowned with success, and on the 3rd

---

* This advice of King Robert is embodied in his political testament
still extant in old Scots metre, as follows :—

> " On fut suld be all Scottis weire
> " Be hyll and mosse themselfe to ware,
> " Let wod for wallis be bow and speire
> " That innymeis do thaim na dreire.
> " *In strait placis gar keipe all stoire,*
> " *And byrn the planen land thaim befoire,*
> " *Thanen sall they pass away in haist*
> " *Quhen that they find naithing bot waist,*
> " With wyllis and wakenin of the nicht
> " And mekill noyes maid on hycht,
> " Thanen sall they turnen with gret affrai
> " As they were chasit with swerd away.
> " This is the counsell and intent
> " Of good King Robert's testament."

October 1357, he and his cousin, Thomas Stewart Earl of Angus, and other great lords, signed a treaty by which they agreed to payment of a ransom of 100,000 marks sterling, the delivery of twenty young men of quality—among them the eldest son of the Stewart—as hostages, and that three out of the eight principal barons of Scotland, including the Stewart himself and his cousin the Earl of Angus, should place themselves in the hands of the King of England.

An interesting episode in David's captivity is preserved in Ashmole's "History of the Order of the Garter," where we learn that at a tournament held at Windsor in 1349 the housings of the Scottish King's charger were of blue velvet, "with a pale of red velvet, and, beneath, *a white rose* embroidered "thereon." This, on the authority of Lord Hailes, is the earliest mention of the *Scottish white rose*, destined in after years to be the party badge of the adherents of the Stewarts. The Scottish "White Rose" would thus appear to have been of much more ancient date than, and to be entirely unconnected with, the white rose of York.

David II. returned to his kingdom and ratified the treaty by which he had obtained his freedom, but, as subsequently transpired, he had secretly bound himself to demolish the Castles of Dalswinton and Durrisdeer (belonging to cousins of his nephew the Stewart) and those of Morton and Dumfries. In 1359 the Stewart was created Earl of Strathearn in reward of his faithful services, but unfortunately the honour seems to have been given more in deference to popular feeling than from sincere regard, as David's whole subsequent career from his return to the throne, preserved for him by his nephew's loyalty, valour, and ability, until the day of his death, is marked by a determined and persistent jealousy of that nephew, his family, and friends. Thomas Stewart, Earl of Angus, notwithstanding his great services both in the field and in negotiating and guaranteeing the treaty by which the King recovered his freedom, was the first to suffer, being thrown into prison on suspicion of instigating the murder of the King's favourite concubine, Catherine Mortimer of Wales. He was confined in the Castle of Dumbarton, where he was attacked by the plague and died in 1361.

Except the quality of personal courage—the possession of which he never failed to prove when occasion arose—King

David Brus possessed none of the great qualities of his illustrious father. His whole life after his return from captivity was given to pleasure and frivolity. His unbounded extravagance led to a small rebellion amongst his nobles, who became exasperated by seeing the sums voluntarily imposed and borne by the country for the purpose of his ransom, squandered instead in Royal extravagance, regardless of the risk of an English war, or the consequences to their sons, hostages in the hands of King Edward for the ransom money—several of whom, as a fact, ultimately died in captivity in England. These feelings at length found vent in a league between the Earls of Douglas and March and the High Stewart with a view to compelling the King to change his counsellors, but David with unusual promptitude saved himself on this occasion by attacking and defeating Douglas, after which the league was dissolved, and the confederate lords returned to their allegiance. The Bond exacted from the Stewart on this occasion, according to Fordun, was under penalty of forfeiting for ever all right and title to the Crown of Scotland as well as to his own inheritances, and of being held a perjured man and a false and dishonoured knight!

Queen Joanna having died shortly before this, David married a second time, and his second Queen, known as Margaret Logy, led to fresh and more serious ruptures between the King and his nobility, and particularly between him and his nephew, the High Stewart.

It is probable that David's notorious vanity and little-mindedness may have been wounded by the influence and measure of popular respect and affection attained by his nephew as the natural result of the great services rendered to his country from the time when, as a lad of sixteen, he fought at Halidon Hill, till, in the prime of manhood, he handed over the government of Scotland to the King. With the exception of about five years—the interval between David's return from France and his capture at the Battle of Durham—the Scots had, for a quarter of a century, been accustomed to regard the Stewart as the head of the State and the centre of all authority, and these habits would no doubt occasionally obtrude themselves unpleasantly on the notice of the actual sovereign. David having no son, the Stewart was, both by birth and by virtue of Brus's Act of Settlement in 1318, the undoubted heir to the Crown, but yielding to his jealousy—not improbably played upon for her own purposes by his new Queen—David in his next Parliament (1364) proposed that the Act of Settlement should be set aside and the Crown of Scotland given to the Duke of Clarence, a son of Edward III. King of England. This humiliating proposal was however indignantly rejected by the Scots Estates, who absolutely refused to listen to the suggestion of an English successor, and who flatly told the incensed King that in addition to being the undoubted Heirs Presumptive to the Crown, "the Stewart and his sons had " proved themselves to be brave men and fit to reign."

David's animosity seems only to have been increased by

this reply. The Acts of Parliament of the time afford indication of a desire on the part of the King to involve his nephew and his friends the Earls of Douglas and March—the leaders of the party opposed to the extravagance of himself and the ambitions of his wife—in the rebellion which had long been simmering in the Highlands. The Hebrides, and the Districts of Athole, Badenoch, Lochaber, and Ross, were in a state of actual disaffection. The barons had defied the Royal authority and refused to pay their share of the ransom money. One of the leading offenders was the Lord of the Isles, who had married the High Stewart's daughter, a relationship which appears to have led King David to obtain an injunction on the Stewart as Lord of Strathearn, on his eldest son John as Lord of Kyle, and on his second son Robert as Lord of Menteith, forbidding them to allow criminals to harbour on their lands or within their jurisdictions.

Whether it was on a charge of some such conduct, or, as is more generally believed, by the malevolent instigation of the Queen, who nourished an implacable enmity to them, the Stewart and his three sons, John, Robert, and Alexander, were in 1366-7 thrown into prison. The prison selected for the Stewart, and at least his third son, Alexander, was the Castle of Lochleven—thus early, ominous of the future, and destined to prove equally inauspicious to his unfortunate descendant Queen Mary. The old accounts of the Chamberlain of Scotland show that the castle at this time underwent repair and fortification for the

P

safe-keeping of the illustrious prisoners. The duration of their confinement is uncertain. It seems probable however that the Stewart himself was not many months in durance, as, while the accounts audited in 1368 show the expense of the maintenance of both himself and his son, those of the following year only deal with the maintenance of Sir Alexander Stewart, from which it may be inferred that his father had either been liberated or removed to another prison. Their liberation was probably not unconnected with the wane of David's affection for his new Queen and his contemplated divorce from her, a change of sentiment calculated to induce kindlier feelings towards her victims, and even perhaps a sense of shame for the manner in which he had rewarded his nephew's loyalty and great services to himself.

The ex-Queen's influence for evil upon the fortunes of the Stewarts did not however end here, and as her history has been much obscured and greatly misrepresented, a short account of her life, as far as her story can now be discovered, will better enable the transactions of this period to be fully understood.

This second Queen of David Brus is generally described as the daughter of a noble family in Perthshire, and as possessed of all the charms of youth and maidenhood at the time of her marriage to that King. Recent research however has completely overturned these earlier accounts of this remarkable woman, and while giving much additional information concerning her, has also deprived her of much of the romance hitherto associated with her.

In the Errol Charter Chest, Mr Riddell, the indefatigable antiquarian expert on Peerage Law already referred to, discovered a solemn bond or agreement dated at Edinburgh in 136— (the last figure being unfortunately undecipherable) between, on the one part, John Kennedy of Dunure, and on the other part, "My most excellent Lady, Lady Margaret, by " the grace of God Queen of Scots" and "her *son* the noble " and powerful John de Logie lord thereof." This Kennedy of Dunure—ancestor of the Earls of Cassilis and Ailsa—was a turbulent and intriguing chieftain of Galloway (which then comprised part of Ayrshire), who had only a short time before been outlawed for his misdeeds. The object of the bond (which however is of minor importance in relation to the present purpose) was plainly to strengthen the Queen's power politically, with a view to her own and her son's aggrandisement, but the great interest which the deed possesses, lies in the facts which may be gathered from it relative to this adventuress who, by the power which she was able to exercise over the facile David by her voluptuous charms,—" voluptatæ " formæ appetitivæ," in the language of Fordun,—gained a position which enabled her to agitate and convulse Scotland for many a day, and to cause much trouble and misery to the Stewarts, who, as next heirs to the Crown, early incurred her animosity.

As has been indicated, it has generally been believed that her maiden name was Logie, and that she was a daughter of the Logies of that ilk, a family of considerable note in Perthshire at that time.

Mr Riddell's discovery showed that, contrary to the general belief, she was neither young nor a maiden when she induced the King to marry her, but he was not able to solve the mystery of her parentage. The publication however of the " Liber Pluscardensis " and other old records, since his time, places it apparently beyond a doubt that her maiden name was Drummond, and that in fact she was the daughter of Sir Malcolm Drummond and aunt of Annabella Drummond, the good Queen of Robert III.

Her first husband, it may be gathered, was John de Logie of Logie in Perthshire, the son and heir of that Sir John de Logie who, according to Fordun, was executed by Brus

in 1320 as a traitor for complicity in the Soulis Conspiracy.
From this marriage she derived the designation of Margaret
Logie, by which she is generally known in history. The date
of her first husband's death is uncertain, some writers maintaining that he was alive in 1362, while Mr Riddell, pointing
to a deed of 1357–8 (now preserved in the Mar Charter Chest),
is of opinion that he must have been then dead, as in the
document in question King David revoked a grant of the
lands of Strongartney in Perthshire which he had made
" *on the suggestion of others*" to " *quondam* John de Logie."
This same Charter goes on to state that these lands had once
been part of the paternal inheritance of the Logies, but, as
King David had now discovered, they had been forfeited by
the father of the said " quondam John de Logie " in the days
of King Robert de Brus, and had by that monarch been conferred as a reward of his valour and fidelity on *Sir John
Menteith* and his spouse Elene de Mar, and their heirs. In
these circumstances King David had no alternative but to recall
his earlier grant and restore the lands of Strongartney to Sir
John Menteith's son—whom he calls " consanguineo nostro,"
his mother, Elene de Mar, being the niece of King Robert de
Brus's first Queen, Isabella de Mar. The designation is of
interest as proving the custom then prevalent of acknowledg-
ing family connections, however slender (as in the present
instance), in order to conciliate and cement those bonds, the
formation of which interest or affection dictated.

King David's first Queen, the Princess Joanna Plantagenet, died on 14th August 1362, and five months later Margaret Logie appears on the scene in a grant made by David (20th January 1363) of £5 yearly to the Dominican Friars of Aberdeen "for the safety of my soul and that of my dear " Margaret de Logy." He does not seem however to have married her till nearly a year later, and the "Scalacronica" (in commenting on the Douglas and Stewart agitation against the Royal extravagance) gives us some indication of the date, and of the relations previously existing between the King and his future wife, by asserting that "this riot being subdued for the " time, the said David took to wife Dame Margaret of Logy, " a lady who had been formerly married, and had already lived " with him," etc. The marriage certainly took place before February 1364, when "Margaret, wife of David Brus," received a safe conduct to visit the shrine of St Thomas of Canterbury.

The infatuated David gave her as dowry, the Customs of the Burghs of Inverkeithing and Aberdeen, as well as the "fermes" of these Burghs and the "fermes" of Kinghorn. She had a grant of the lands of Kinclevin, Abernethy, Rate, Fardell, Lethendry, etc., together with the Abthania of Dull (of which her youngest brother, Maurice, ancestor of the Drummonds of Megginch, was "Bailie," and which she conveyed to her son), and she also obtained the lands of Stobhall, Cargill, and Kinloch, which she conveyed to her nephew Malcolm Drummond. In 1366, King David by an act of flagrant injustice, gave to her son John de Logie the lands in Annandale which King Robert de Brus had bestowed on his brave nephew, Randolph Earl of Moray. To these lands, though at the time in the occupation of the English, Randolph's daughter, the wife of the Earl of March, was heir, and it was not improbably to strengthen themselves against the resentment of that Earl, and his friends the High Stewart and the Earl of Douglas, that the Queen and her son entered into the bond with Kennedy of Dunure already referred to.

Her extravagance, added to that of the King, was a source of constant annoyance to the nobles, who saw with high displeasure the money which ought to have been devoted to paying off the King's ransom, lavished in pilgrimages to England, and in the personal gratification of the King and Queen. Among other extravagances to which the accounts bear witness is the cost of the erection of alabaster tombs for herself and King David at Dunfermline, an expenditure destined to be useless, as David was buried at Holyrood, while her own grave is unknown.

The fascination she exercised over the weak King appears to have been almost purely sensual, and was accordingly shortlived. But while it lasted, she exercised her arts and undoubtedly great talents and abilities towards the aggrandisement of her son and herself. For the former, in addition to the lands already referred to, she obtained soon after her marriage a charter of the Thanedom of Thanadas (probably Tannadyce) in Forfarshire, with the reversion of Glamis, part of the Royal property. In 1367 he appears in an English passport as "John de Logie "de Scotia," travelling with a retinue of twelve horsemen.

On what pretext David divorced her is uncertain, though the "Liber Pluscardensis" seems to indicate that the step was not unconnected with an attempt to palm off a false heir on the kingdom. Could this have been successfully accomplished, her power and influence would of course have been greatly strengthened and prolonged, and the attempt may afford some explanation of the dislike she entertained towards the Stewart and his sons, as next heirs to the Crown, and of her desire to get them conveniently disposed of in prison.

However this may be, the ex-Queen was very far from quietly accepting the decree of divorce which David succeeded in persuading the Scottish Church to pronounce against her, and with a resolution and courage which compels an admiration altogether unmerited by her general conduct, she set out for Avignon—then the seat of the Roman Pontiff—and appealed to the Pope for a reversal of the decree of divorce. This suit she prosecuted with the utmost determination long after her husband King David's death in 1371, to the great annoyance and disturbance of his successor King Robert II. and the Scottish people generally, over whom threats of excommunication were continually dangled *in terrorem*. By what arts and wiles, beyond her personal charms and address, she so gained on the Pope and Cardinals cannot now be ascertained, but it is certain that she at length succeeded in her desire, and obtained from the Pope a reversal of the verdict given by the Scottish Church. It is however significant that in 1372 she obtained a loan of 1500 merks from certain English merchants at Avignon, and that in 1374, under the designation of "the *wife* of our dear brother David Brus," she obtained from Edward III.—the brother of her predecessor on the Scottish throne—permission to reside in England for two years. It is therefore by no means improbable that her protracted suit before the Roman Court, which, especially after King David's death must have been inspired largely by vindictive considerations, was aided and abetted by the politic King of England with a view to embarrassing the new King of Scots and his government generally. Her influence with the Popes Urban and Gregory, who successively dealt with her suit, had a most malign effect on Scottish affairs, especially on the advent of a new dynasty, and that, one to which the ex-Queen had so bitter and deadly an enmity.

On the death of David Brus in 1371, his nephew, Robert the High Stewart of Scotland, ascended the throne as Robert II., and at once found himself confronted with the troubles raised by this ambitious woman from abroad. Various letters passed between him and the King of France on the subject, Robert entreating his brother Monarch, and even remonstrating with him for failing, to use his influence with the Pope to put an end to the persecution to which he and the people of Scotland were being subjected by threats of Papal excommunication. Her machinations were however closed by her sudden death in 1374-75, and King Robert then found himself free to attend to the affairs of his kingdom unmolested by the clerical terrors which had so long hung over him.

His coronation had taken place on 26th March 1371, on which occasion, following the example of his illustrious grandfather, he nominated his son John, Earl of Carrick and Stewart of Scotland, as the heir to the throne. King Robert had now reached the age of fifty-five, and the activity, promptitude, resolution, and military fire which had distinguished him in youth, had toned down into a gentler and more peaceful disposition. For the next twenty years, till his death in 1390, at the ripe age of seventy-four, his efforts were directed towards securing peace and good government for his people, the benefits of which, with a wisdom unfortunately too advanced for his day and generation, he saw would be far greater, more real and enduring, than any chance victories or successes in war, which would indeed be likely only to bring corresponding calamities in their train by inciting the enemy to revenge previous defeats. In these efforts however he was ill-seconded by a turbulent nobility much too independent of the Crown to permit of the personal views or wishes of the Sovereign having the weight to which they were entitled. The old King therefore had the disappointment and mortification of seeing his wisest and best endeavours defeated, and a succession of border raids and retaliatory expeditions continually disturbing the peace of the country.

The recapitulation in detail of these events is more properly matter of national history than of biography, but some notice of the chief incidents between his succession and his death will not be out of place, and may even be judged necessary to complete the story of his life.

In 1371, King Robert took steps to renew the league with France, in accordance with which the French Monarch engaged to withstand all attempts on the part of the English to alter the succession to the Crown of Scotland, while it was mutually agreed that no subject of either country should serve in the armies of England.

The following year, 1372, is noteworthy for the passing of severe statutes against murderers and their abettors, while the nation was enjoined that no mandate against the common course of law was in future to be obeyed, under whatever seal it might be issued.

One of the most important events in the history of the Stewarts, and indeed in the political history of Scotland, took place in the following year (1373), when King Robert executed a fresh settlement of the Crown, and obtained its formal ratification by Parliament.

By this deed, the purport of which is little known in the present day and its significance still less realized, King Robert entailed the Crown of Scotland on the sons, *nominatim*, of his first marriage, and on the *heirs male* of their bodies, respectively, with remainder in the same way to the sons of his second marriage and the heirs male of *their* bodies, failing whom the Crown was to go to the true and legal heirs of the Stewarts whomsoever. By this statute, as will be seen, the Crown of Scotland was strictly entailed in the male line, and while a single legitimate male descendant of Robert II. existed, no female could have ascended the throne. As a matter of fact, the succession only opened to Mary Queen of Scots and her descendants, through the entire failure of legitimate male heirs of any of the numerous sons of King Robert II.—the last heirs male of that monarch being Mary's father, King James V., and his cousin the Duke of Albany, both of whom died within a short time of each other. The last "remainder" in King Robert's Act of Settlement then came into operation, and the infant Mary succeeded her father on the Scottish throne in virtue of the provision in question, that in the event of the failure of the entire male line of King Robert II., the Crown should go to his heirs-at-law, "veri et legitimi heredes de " sanguine et parentela regali." The succession of Queen Mary has therefore the effect of proving that within, roughly, 200 years of their ascending the throne, the male line of the Royal branch of the Stewarts had become extinct, and the male representation of the race would thereupon revert to the Stuarts of Darnley, the senior representatives of Sir John Stewart of Bonkyl. As is well known, Queen Mary married Lord Darnley, and in their son, King James VI., was therefore united the representation of the direct lines of the Stewarts, both male and female.

The next few years seem to have been comparatively quiet and unimportant, as little or nothing is recorded worthy of special note.

In 1377 various border raids of more or less importance took place, in which the English seem to have had much the worst of the encounters, and in the next year the English commerce was severely harried by Mercer in revenge for the imprisonment of his father, a French merchant, by the English. In the same year also, 1378, the strong Castle of Berwick was surprised by an esquire, Alexander Ramsay, who with only forty men succeeded in effecting an entrance, killed the commander, and captured the Castle. This insult to the English arms however brought the Earl of Northumberland on the scene, and notwithstanding a spirited attempt of the Scots to render assistance, the small garrison was overpowered and put to the sword—Ramsay alone being spared. On the other hand, Northumberland's troops, joined to those of the Earl of Nottingham, having entered Scotland, suffered severe loss at the hands of Archibald Douglas, Lord of Galloway, and the King's sons, Robert Earl of Fife and Menteith, and Walter Earl of Athole, who overpowered a strong advance party under Musgrave, the Governor of Berwick, in which encounter Musgrave, his son, and many knights and squires were captured, and afterwards carried prisoners to Edinburgh.

The next few years present the same story of more or less continual border raids and broken truces, and in 1384 the Duke of Lancaster and the Earls of Northumberland and Nottingham entered Scotland at the head of a large army to punish the Scots for their temerity and their spoliation of the northern counties of England. Though they ravaged and burned the country before them up to the walls of the capital, they were at length forced to retire with but little plunder to reward them, a step which, as usual, was the signal for an immediate inroad by a Scottish host, which sacked and devastated the lands of Northumberland, Nottingham, and the Mowbrays, in retaliation. In such expeditions, the advantage lay all with the poorer country. The houses of the people of Scotland were then only huts, consisting of four or five posts, dry stone, or, more commonly, turf walls, and roofs of straw or branches, while a cow's hide, suspended from the roof, did duty for a door. If burned—as they commonly were—the loss was slight and easily remedied, and as the cattle and more valuable goods of the inhabitants were generally moved into the forests on the approach of the enemy, an English raid effected little, either in destruction or in capture of spoil, compared with the loss and havoc which accompanied a Scottish raid on the wealthier southern country.

In 1384, William Earl of Douglas, brought Teviotdale, which had been in English hands since the Battle of Durham in 1346, again under the subjection of the Scottish Crown, and in the following year his great relative Archibald Douglas, Lord of Galloway, captured Lochmaben Castle and razed it to the ground.

The year 1385 was signalized by the landing in Scotland of a large body of French knights and their followers under John de Vienne, Admiral of France, to assist the Scots against the common enemy of England. The auxiliaries proved more troublesome than valuable however. Their gallantries irritated King Robert and his nobles, while their petulance and unconcealed disdain of the poverty of the country frequently brought them into conflict with the common people. Little was accomplished beyond the usual raid and counter raid, a mode of warfare which the French despised, failing to realize the true circumstances of the two enemies, and they at length returned home, to the relief and satisfaction both of themselves and their allies.

In 1387, Sir William Douglas of Nithsdale, a son-in-law of King Robert, invaded Ireland with a force of about 500, attacked and captured the town of Carlingford, and held it to ransom. This ransom the inhabitants agreed to pay, but having sent secretly for assistance to Dundalk, treacherously attacked Douglas in overwhelming force. The Scots however after an obstinate fight won the day, and to repay the treachery, burned the town of Carlingford to the ground, harried the Castle, and sailed for home with fifteen Irish vessels loaded with spoil.

The following year witnessed the great Battle of Otterburn, the particulars of which are too familiar to need recapitulation here. As is well known, the English were totally defeated, and their leader Hotspur Percy and many other Knights captured or killed. On the other hand the Scots, though victorious, had to mourn the death of their brave leader, James, the second Earl of Douglas, while the King also lost in the Earl a favourite son-in-law, together with other friends, including Sir Walter Stewart and Sir James Stewart of Agurstone.

On the death of this great prop of his throne—the Earl of Douglas being by far the most powerful noble of the time— King Robert seems to have abandoned all hope of governing peaceably, and, retiring to his Castle of Dundonald, he entrusted the reins of Government to his sons, and spent the remaining years of his life in seclusion, dying at Dundonald on 13th May 1390, at the age of seventy-four. He was buried in the Abbey of Scone, and in the national accounts of the year 1394 there appears an entry of £6, 13s. 4d. paid for a stone from the Church of St John at Perth, and 4s. for its carriage to Scone, for the King's tomb. It may here also be observed that in the accounts of the year 1379 there is an entry of £12 paid to " Andrew the painter " for an alabaster stone for the tomb of Queen Elizabeth Mure, King Robert's first wife.

King Robert the Second was twice married, first to the beautiful Elizabeth More or Mure of Rowallan, and secondly to Euphemia Ross, the widow of Thomas Randolph Earl of Moray.

The facts connected with his first marriage have been grossly distorted by various historians—notably Buchanan and Boece—who, for their own purposes, have sought to attach an unmerited stigma not only to King Robert himself, but to his issue by this union. According to them, the King's marriage with Elizabeth Mure did not take place until after the death of his other wife, Euphemia Ross, whose children consequently were the legal heirs of the Crown from which they were excluded by their father's partiality for (as those writers allege) his former concubine and her illegitimate issue. This calumny was first refuted by Sir Lewis Stewart, the celebrated advocate of the time of Charles I., and he was followed by the Earl of Cromarty, Dalrymple of Hailes, Father Hay, and others, who, quoting Acts of Parliament and other State documents, proved that the stories circulated by their predecessors could not be true. The actual state of matters remained uncertain until the end of last century, when it was the good fortune of Mr Andrew Stuart of Torrance and Castlemilk—himself descended from one of the oldest branches of the Stewarts—to make discoveries in the Papal Archives at Rome which have settled once and for ever the calumnies regarding King Robert, his wife Elizabeth Mure, and their children. In the course of other antiquarian researches, Mr Stuart, in 1789, discovered in the above repositories the original Papal Dispensations authorizing both of the marriages of King Robert, he and his wife in each instance having been within the forbidden degrees of consanguinity or affinity as then interpreted by the Church—degrees so comprehensive as even to preclude marriage between descendants of *godparents* and *godchildren* for one or more generations.

The research of still more recent enquirers has brought additional facts to light whereby we are able to piece together pretty accurately the true story of these incidents in King Robert's life.

From a Papal dispensation granted on 12th October 1344, it appears that Elizabeth Mure, when about eleven years of age, had been contracted in marriage to Hugh de Gifford. The marriage had never been consummated, but the mere contract was held to be a bar to her marriage with any other person until the previous paper union had been dissolved by the Church. It is interesting in this connection to note that Buchanan's story about Elizabeth having married one Gifford after she had borne children to the Stewart, is thus proved not to have been the mere fable it was long believed to be, but rather an ignorant, if not even malicious, perversion or mis-statement of fact. The contract between Gifford and the future Queen was dissolved in 1344, but further impediments to regular marriage next turned up in the fact that the Stewart and his intended wife were related in the fourth degree of consanguinity, and that the lady was further related, in the third degree of consanguinity to another lady between whom and the Stewart there had been relations which, by the consistorial laws, precluded his marriage to her relative without the intervention of the Papal authority. Both of these impediments were also removed by another Papal dispensation granted in 1347, and the marriage took place shortly thereafter.

Queen Elizabeth Mure must have died before 1355, for in that year the Stewart obtained another Papal dispensation, for his second marriage, viz., to Euphemia Ross, the widow of the Earl of Moray.

These documents have a double interest, enabling us as they do to understand much of the apparent wickedness of the age, as it is clear that married life had little security when either spouse lay exposed to actions of divorce on the ground of alleged irregularities in the marriage through the existence of one of the numerous impediments referred to, and the same impediments to regular marriage were no doubt a not unfruitful source of that licentiousness of which the age stands accused. The troubled conscience of humanity must, under such conditions, have proved a rich harvest-field for a Church already wealthy beyond belief.

The chief importance however attaching to these dispensations is the proof they afford that King Robert had been regularly married to his first wife seven or eight years before his second marriage, and, as a dispensation would not have been granted for a second marriage during the subsistence of an earlier union, the dispensation of 1355 also proves that Elizabeth Mure must then have been dead—a fact which conclusively disposes of Buchanan's other slander that the marriage of the King to Elizabeth Mure did not take place till after the death of Euphemia Ross.

But while it is indisputable that a regular marriage took place, it is equally clear from the date of the dispensation and the necessity for it, that the children of Elizabeth Mure were born out of *regular* wedlock. The Papal dispensation however states that King Robert and his wife had been ignorant that there existed between them some of those distant, and in this as in many other cases startling, "relationships" which the consistorial laws of the times interposed as barriers to marriage. In any case the Papal dispensation of 1347 specially legalizing the union and legitimating the issue, disposes of the slanders of Buchanan and other writers, and there is indeed no doubt whatever that at the time, the sons of King Robert by Elizabeth Mure were regarded, and so appear in the Acts of Parliament and in official deeds, as the first heirs of the Stewart of Scotland, and as such entitled to precedence over those of his second wife Euphemia Ross.

The children of the first marriage were—

(1) John, created Earl of Carrick and Lord of Kyle by David II., and who in due course succeeded his father on the throne under the title of " Robert "III." in deference to a popular superstition that the name of John was unfortunate to Royalty.

(2) Sir Walter Stewart, who married Isabel (or Elizabeth, for the names seem to have been frequently used interchangeably), Countess of Fife. He seems to have died about 1362, as his name does not appear on the Rolls after that date. His widow, in 1371, acknowledged his brother Robert as her nearest legal heir, both in right of his wife, the Countess of Menteith, and in virtue of an agreement between her husband, Sir Walter Stewart, and herself.

(3) Robert, Earl of Fife and Menteith, Duke of Albany and Regent of Scotland.

(4) Alexander, Earl of Buchan and Lord of Badenoch.

(5) Margaret, who, by dispensation granted 14th June 1350, married the Lord of the Isles. Their son Donald was a hostage for his father to King David II. in 1369. The date of the dispensation (1350) plainly proves her the daughter of the first marriage.

(6) Elizabeth, who married Sir Thomas Hay the Constable of Scotland, and thus became ancestress of

the Hays, Earls of Errol and Hereditary Constables of Scotland.

(7) ——————— name unknown, who married Sir John Keith, eldest son of Sir William Keith, the Marischal of Scotland, as is proved by a charter of 17th January 1373-74, in which King Robert II. grants to "our dear son John de Keith" all the lands of his father Sir William Keith. The son of this marriage is described by Wynton as "a mychty "man" in 1395, in which year he besieged his aunt at Fyvie, and then attacked her husband Sir David Lindsay at Kirk of Bourtie. If the son was "a "mychty man" in 1395, the mother must almost necessarily have been a daughter of King Robert by his first wife.

(8) Marjory, who married John Dunbar Earl of March. The dispensation for this marriage (11th June 1370) points out Elizabeth Mure as her mother also.

(9) Isabel, who married, by dispensation dated 24th September 1371, James Earl of Douglas, the hero of Otterburn. After Douglas's death in 1388, she married (1390) Sir John Edmonstone. She had no children by her first marriage, but left one son by her second husband. She seems to have died 1409-10, as in the Rolls of that year she is designated "quondam Comitisse de Douglas."

(10) Jean, said by Hume of Godscroft to be the daughter
of Elizabeth Mure. She married Sir John Lyon,
who was soon afterwards created Great Chamberlain of Scotland and Lord of Kinghorn. After much
public service Sir John was slain in a private
quarrel by Lord Lindsay of Crawford, the King's
nephew—son of his sister Egidia. For this lawless
deed Lord Lindsay incurred the high displeasure of
King Robert, who took his young grandson John,
Lord Glamis, under his special care, brought him up
at his Court, and forbade anyone to interfere either
with him or his property under severe penalties.
From this John, Lord Glamis, descend in a direct
line the Earls of Strathmore and Kinghorn, Lords
Glamis.

By his second marriage King Robert had—

(1) David, Earl of Strathearn.

(2) Walter, Earl of Athole.

(3) ———— (called indifferently Jean, Katherine, or
Elizabeth) who married Sir David Lindsay of
Glenesk. The date of the marriage is unknown,
but certainly was not later than 1384, in which year
he is described in a Charter as "The King's son."
She is generally stated to have been a daughter of
Elizabeth Mure, but this could not be unless she
was very much older than her husband, who seems

to have been only eighteen at the time of his marriage.

(4) Egidia or Giles is also usually described as the daughter of Elizabeth Mure, but if so, she must have been considerably over thirty at the time of her marriage to Sir William Douglas in 1387. As the supposition is entirely inconsistent with the accounts of her charms and fascinations, it is more probable that she was, as here stated, a daughter of the second marriage. The fame of the beauty of this Princess spread even to the continent, and the King of France is said to have been so enamoured of her even by hearsay, that he obtained a miniature portrait of her, and sued for her hand. She however gave her heart to a Scottish knight, Sir William Douglas of Nithsdale already mentioned, a natural son of Archibald, Lord of Galloway, but a worthy representative of his illustrious grandfather "The Good Lord James" of Douglas, and inferior to none of his renowned name and race in valour and military talent. Sir William Douglas was indeed generally admitted to be the most gallant knight in Europe of his day. He acted as the right hand man of his father, the grim Lord of Galloway, and was no less beloved, for his kind heart, than feared by his enemies for his courage

s

and valour. His thirst for glory however led to his early death. After scourging the English and Irish pirates who infested the western coasts of Scotland—as we have already seen—he sailed for the continent with a body of Scottish Knights, and is reported to have been given the command of the Teutonic fleet, which so displeased a rival—the English Lord Clifford—that he challenged him to single combat, but is alleged to have basely procured his assassination before the appointed day. There appears to be no doubt that the brave Sir William Douglas fell by the knife of an assassin at Dantzig, but that Lord Clifford had any share in his death is by no means so well ascertained. His only child by the fair Egidia was a daughter (also named Egidia) who married Sir Alexander Stewart, son of Sir Robert Stewart of Durrisdeer, a descendant of James the High Stewart, grandfather of King Robert II.

Sir Robert Stewart of Durrisdeer himself was one of the companions of Sir William Douglas in the above expedition, and in the papers in the Hamilton Charter-chest reported on by the Historical MS. Commission, is a copy of a Bond granted at Dantzig by a Sir James Douglas (believed to be one of the Douglasses of Dalkeith) for a sum of money lent him by Sir Robert Stewart in which the borrower acknowledges the debt and promises to repay it, under the penalty in case of failure of never more wearing the arms of a Knight unless with his creditor's consent.

King Robert had also several children born out of wedlock, viz. :—

(1) Sir John Stewart, on whom he conferred the office of Heritable Sheriff of Bute (salary £6, 13s. 4d. per annum!) and from whom descend in a direct male line the Stuarts, Earls and Marquises of Bute, the Earls of Wharncliffe, and the numerous cadets of those noble houses.

(2) Thomas Stewart, Archdeacon of St Andrews, whose name appears in the Customs Accounts from 1384 to 1402, and in an English safe-conduct in 1395. In 1401 he was elected Bishop of St Andrews, but declined the office, being, according to Bower, a man of "the most modest spirit and dovelike simplicity."

(3) Alexander Stewart, Canon of Glasgow, who, as "fratre nostro," witnesses a Charter by the Duke of Albany in 1407.

(4) Sir John Stewart of Dundonald (the red Stewart), Lord of Burley, who about 1402 succeeded the celebrated Sir William Stewart of Jedworth—ancestor of the Earls of Galloway—as Clerk of the Audit to the King. He appears in this capacity, and as an Auditor, down till King James's return from

captivity, and was knighted on the occasion of his nephew's coronation. Along with many other nobles he was soon afterwards thrown into prison, but was shortly released and appointed Captain of the Castle of Dumbarton, in which capacity he was acting when the Castle was attacked in 1426 by his cousin Sir James "Mhor" Stewart, son of Murdach Duke of Albany. Sir John Stewart was among those killed in the attack. He had married Elizabeth, daughter of William Lord Graham, and seems to be the "John Stewart" referred to by King Robert in a charter (15th January 1382-83) of the lands of "Ballachys Invernate and Muckirsy in Kinclevin" as "dilecto filio nostro genito inter nos et dilectam "nostram Moram."

(5) Sir Alexander Stewart of Inverlunan.

(6) Sir James Stewart of Kinfauns.

(7) Sir John Stewart of Cardney.

The mother of the three last named knights was Mariote de Cardney, daughter of Sir John Cardney of that ilk, and sister of Robert Cardney, Bishop of Dunkeld. She received lands from King Robert in the counties of Kinross and Aberdeen, with remainder to her three sons above named, and they also had remainder in the grant of lands to their half-brother, the red Stewart of Dundonald. Various entries appear in the Exchequer Rolls of the time relative to expenses paid on her account.

On 3rd January 1377-78, Sir Alexander Stewart received a grant of the lands of Inverlunan in Forfarshire, with remainder to his brothers James and John, and five years later these were further augmented by a grant of the lands of Lunan in Forfarshire and Pitfour in Buchan.

On 25th December 1372, Sir James Stewart received a grant of the reversion of an annuity from the lands of Abernethy then enjoyed by Margaret Stewart Countess of Angus, and on 15th January 1382-83, when his brother Alexander obtained the lands of Pitfour, he obtained the lands of Kinfauns, Rate, and Mill of Forteviot, with remainder to his brothers Alexander and John. In his youth he seems to have studied at St Andrews along with Gilbert de Hay, son of Sir John Hay and Margaret Stewart of Railstoun. Their education was supervised by the Archbishop of St Andrews, and the expense was paid by the King, as appears from the Exchequer Rolls of 1384 and 1386. His name, and that of his brother John, occurs in various other Rolls as receiving gifts from the King, and in 1398 Sir James Stewart of Kinfauns figures in a much less creditable or agreeable a position as a prisoner— though his offence is not stated—in the Castle of Edinburgh by orders of his brother, King Robert III., the expense of his maintenance (£24) being paid out of the Burgh customs.

On 15th January 1382-83, Sir John Stewart received a grant of the lands of Kinclevin, Arntully, Tullibelyn, and

Dulmernok, with remainder to Alexander and James. He studied at Paris, and the expenses of his education appear in the Exchequer Rolls of the time, as paid to his uncle Robert of Cardney. On 12th February 1399 he received from his brother, King Robert III., a grant of the two Cardneys in Perthshire—the ancestral lands of his mother's family. He was knighted on the occasion of King James' coronation, and the lands of Cardney and Arntully were long in the possession of his descendants.

King Robert's grant of the lands of Cardney is said to have contained a reversion in favour of a fourth son of Mariote de Cardney, viz. :—

> (8) Walter Stewart, who, if this be so, was probably born after the earlier grants had been made. The lands of Pitfour (the property originally of Sir Alexander Stewart) and those of Burley (the property previously of Sir John of Dundonald) were certainly, in the next generation, possessed by a Sir Walter Stewart, who appears on an assize in 1439, but whether he was a fourth son of Marion de Cardney, or only a grandson, is uncertain. He must have died about 1454, as his lands were then in the Crown's hands, and he seems to have left no male issue, as in 1477 his elder daughter Egidia Stewart, then a widow, conveyed her half of the lands of Pitfour to John Anderson, Burgess of Aberdeen.

The only two of King Robert's children whose history will be here dealt with are Alexander Earl of Buchan, and David Earl of Strathearn. The latter died before his father, and the former did not long survive him, while the history of their brothers can more appropriately be treated in illustration of the times of the succeeding sovereigns in whose reigns they played a prominent part.

Alexander, Earl of Buchan, in March 1371, received a charter of the district of Badenoch and the Castle of Lochindorb, forfeited by the powerful family of Comyn through adherence to Baliol and the English interest. On 17th June 1371 he obtained the lands of Strathavon, and on 7th October 1372 was made Lieutenant for his father King Robert, of the whole district north of Morayshire, and Justiciar north of the Forth. In 1376-77, and again in 1379, he received grants of other lands in the Counties of Banff, Aberdeen, Inverness, and Sutherland. He married Euphemia, daughter and heir of William, Earl of Ross, by whom he came into possession of vast estates throughout Scotland. The islands of Skye and the Lews, lands in Athole, in Fife, in Galloway, in Caithness, and Sutherland, thus came into his possession, and the Countess also resigned her Earldom in his favour. By descent from a younger daughter of John Comyn Earl of Buchan, the Countess also inherited half of the lands of that Earldom (known as the Barony of Kynedward) and these, on her marriage, she also resigned to the King, who reconveyed them in 1382 to her and to her husband, bestowing also on the latter the title of Earl of Buchan, under which designation he is usually known.

He seems however to have been a turbulent and unruly noble, and, to other vices, to have joined ingratitude both to his father and his wife. The two sobriquets under which he has been handed down in history, "Alexander Mhor Mac-an-Righ" (Big Alexander, the King's son) and "The Wolf of Badenoch," by all accounts fittingly portray his appearance and disposition. Like his father King Robert (and indeed apparently all that Monarch's children), he was a man of splendid physical proportions, but, while endowed with a full share of the family courage, seems to have possessed few or none of his father's better qualities.

Notwithstanding his vast estates, he appears in the accounts of 1381 and 1384 as in debt to Archibald Douglas, Lord of Galloway, which burdens his father then paid off. In the former year too, the rent of the lands of Strathnairn, leased to him by Sir David de Lindsay, was in default and was paid out of the Dundee Customs. In 1384 he is found defying the Custumars of Inverness, and shipping his wool without payment of duty. In 1389 his misdeeds seem to have cost him his office of Justiciar, of which he was that year deprived. On 2nd November 1389 he was ordained by the Bishop of Moray and Ross to live with his wife, under penalty of £200—a command to which he paid no heed. How far we are justified in believing the stories which have been handed down, of his violence, lawlessness, oppression, and licentiousness, or how far they have their origin in the rancour of the monkish historians against whose class and profession "the Wolf of Badenoch" carried on continual war, it is impossible now to say. These tales represent him as leading a life of licence, and making his name a terror throughout the whole district of Badenoch and the adjacent counties. But while the picture is no doubt somewhat overdrawn, sufficient is known to render it extremely probable that the charges were not altogether groundless. Judged by modern standards at least, the Earl of Buchan displayed an utter disregard of law and order, culminating at length in murder, fire-raising, and sacrilege in carrying "red ruin" through the Church lands and property.

From whatever cause arising—whether, as some allege, from resentment of priestly interference in regard to his neglect of his wife (to whom he was unfaithful and with whom he would not live), or, by other accounts, because of a dispute as to the right to certain lands—a feud had been smouldering for some years between him and the Bishop of Moray. While his father lived, respect for the old King seems to have kept the fiery Earl somewhat within bounds, but within

T

a month of King Robert's death, the temper of the Wolf of Badenoch broke out in uncontrolled violence. He invaded and occupied certain lands claimed by the Church, and, ignoring all protests, retained violent possession. The Bishop's complaints and threats, the haughty temporal baron treated with contempt and defiance. The prince of the Church in an ill-advised moment retaliated with spiritual thunders, and passed sentence of excommunication against the Earl of Buchan and all his retainers and supporters. Thereupon the tempest of Alexander's wrath burst on the prelate who had ventured to excommunicate a King's son. With a temerity and utter disregard of consequences, unparalleled at a time when the Church exercised undisputed and almost irresistible sway over the minds and superstitions of the laity, the Earl of Buchan assembled his household, and, accompanied by his natural sons, broke in on the Church lands, and (May 1390) burned the town of Forres, the choir of the church, and the Archdeacon's house. Unsated even by this revenge, or possibly exasperated anew by fresh episcopal fulminations, he, in the following month, attacked the seat of the Bishop himself, burned the town of Elgin to the ground, and gave the churches and the other ecclesiastical property to the flames. In this general conflagration were consumed the Cathedral—"the "mirror of the country and the glory of the kingdom"—the Church of St Giles, the Hospital of Maison Dieu, and eighteen houses of the Canons in the College of Elgin.

The result of these proceedings is somewhat obscure. By some writers it is alleged that the Earl, not content with thus taking the law into his own hands,—for which he may have persuaded himself that his authority as Lieutenant for his father, lately dead, was perhaps sufficient warrant,— proceeded to Perth to lay his complaint before the King, but was promptly arrested and thrown into prison, from which he was not released until he had done abject penance for his sacrilegious misdeeds. There is however no actual proof of this, unless it is to be assumed from the inscription on his tombstone in the Choir of Dunkeld Cathedral, where the fierce Wolf of Badenoch lies buried—" Hic Jacet Dominus " Alexander Senescallus, Comes de Buchan et Dominus de " Badenagh *bonæ memoriæ*, qui obiit 20 die mensis Februarii " Anno: Dom: 1394."

The Wolf of Badenoch left no lawful issue, but by his con-cubine, Mariote de Athyn, was survived by five natural sons.

(1) Sir Alexander Stewart.

(2) Sir Andrew Stewart.

From these brothers descend many of the Athole Stewarts.

(3) Duncan Stewart.

(4) Sir Walter Stewart of Strathdoun and Kincardine, ancestor of the Stewarts of Drumin, Kilmachlie, Auchlunkart, and the Banffshire Stewarts.

(5) Sir James Stewart of Fortingall, ancestor of the cele-brated Stewarts of Garth and their numerous cadets.

Duncan is said to have been the leader of a band of Highland Caterans, who raided Angus in 1391. Of James little is known, and Andrew and Walter only appear at all importantly, in connection with their eldest brother, Sir Alexander, by far the most illustrious of the Wolf's sons.

He also is said to have begun his career as a leader of freebooters, and to have instigated an attack on the Queen's brother, Sir Malcolm Drummond, in which Sir Malcolm was slain. Shortly afterwards, Sir Alexander Stewart attacked the Castle of Kildrummy, in which Sir Malcolm's widow was residing, stormed the Castle, carried off the lady by force, and married her—actions which afford a vivid picture of the times and the powerlessness of the Crown to right wrongs even where Royalty was itself nearly interested. The wife thus won was Isabella Douglas, sister of James, Earl of Douglas who fell at Otterburn, and daughter of William, Earl of Douglas and Mar. On her brother's death the Douglas honours were claimed by, and granted to, his kinsman Archibald the Grim, Lord of Galloway, but the Earldom of Mar descended to the late Earl's sister, the wife of Sir Malcolm Drummond. She also inherited two-thirds of her brother's hereditary pension of 200 marks, and her terce of the annuity of £40 enjoyed by her late husband, Sir Malcolm Drummond.

Notwithstanding this rough wooing the marriage does not seem to have been unhappy, and Sir Alexander Stewart's habits changing, with his fortunes, for the better, his youthful excesses were more than compensated by the steady valour and loyalty of his later years. The Countess conferred on him a liferent of her Earldom of Mar, which his uncle King Robert III. confirmed. "Sua wes yis Stewart for his Bounteis "Beltit Erle of twa Counteis"*—nor did he prove either ungrateful for or unworthy of such promotion.

In revenge of the captivity of his cousin Prince James, he fitted up ships, and infesting the coast between Berwick and Newcastle, preyed on the commerce of the enemy, destroying many English merchantmen.

In 1406 he distinguished himself in a passage of arms in England with Edward Earl of Kent, and two years later, seeking an outlet for his martial ardour which peace at the time denied him at home, he carried his arms abroad, and passing to the Continent with a company of 80 Scottish knights and their followers, rendered material assistance to the Duke of Burgundy against the insurrectionaries, at the Battle of Liege, which was largely won by his valour, skill, and counsel. In this expedition he was accompanied by his younger brother Sir Andrew Stewart, who was knighted by the Duke of Burgundy for his services, and who afterwards received from the Earl of Mar the lands of Sandhalgh and Culquharry. Sir Andrew, it may here be said, also seems to have settled down into a respectable landed proprietor,

---

* *i.e.*, Mar and Garrioch (Winton's "Chronicle").

and in 1427-28 appears in the National Accounts as selling 180 sheep (designated " Mutonibus ") to the King.

The Countess of Mar died in 1408, and Sir Alexander Stewart during his absence abroad married a lady of the Low Countries. This second wife, according to Pussendorff in his " History of Europe," was Jacqueline, Countess of Holland, Zealand, and Friesland, in right of whom Sir Alexander Stewart is stated by the same writer to have claimed the Earldom of Holland, and, being denied, to have fought and defeated the Hollanders at sea.

In 1411 rebellion broke out in the Highlands. Alexander Earl of Ross, dying in 1406, left an only daughter as his heir. Being sickly and in weak health she took the veil, resigning her Earldom in favour of her cousin John Stewart Earl of Buchan, son of Robert Duke of Albany. The Earldom was however, on her father's death, claimed by the Lord of the Isles who had married the sister of the late Earl. Assembling an army of 10,000 men at Inverness, he marched south, carrying destruction as he went. His course was however opposed by Sir Alexander Stewart Earl of Mar, at the head of the citizens of Aberdeen and the gentry of Angus and Mearns. On the " red field of Harlaw " a desperate battle was fought (24th July 1411), in which, though greatly outnumbered, the Earl was victorious, at least to the extent of holding the field and compelling the island lord to retreat. On this occasion the Earl of Mar was accompanied by his brother Sir Walter Stewart, and probably also by Sir Andrew. Large numbers were slain on both sides, and the battle indeed proved absolutely disastrous to many of the lowland families, some of whom lost every male scion of their race on the field.

The valour of the Earl of Mar and his troops however had gained time for the Regent to assemble an army with which he marched into Ross and subdued the Highlanders. It is noteworthy in this connection, as disproving the accusation of avarice frequently brought against the Duke of Albany, that he bore the whole cost of these expeditions himself, and was never reimbursed for his expense. He also paid the Earl of Mar's personal expenses, and rewarded his services with an annuity of £200 from the Customs of Aberdeen. To the Earl was also entrusted the task of superintending the re-building of the Castle of Inverness on an enlarged scale, in order more effectually to overawe the Highlanders. The work extended over several years—the cost for the rebuilding, garrisoning, and provisioning of the Castle being £650!

In 1416 the Earl of Mar again appears fitting out and victualling ships sent against the Islanders of the North; and the same year, along with his uncle Walter Stewart Earl of Athole, and his cousins Lord Murdach Stewart and John Stewart Earl of Buchan (the sons of his uncle Robert, Duke of Albany and Governor of Scotland), he was appointed a Commissioner to negotiate the release of his cousin King James I.

In 1420, Alexander, Earl of Mar, entered into an agreement of "service and retinue," as it was called, with the Duke of Albany, and on the latter's death he renewed the league with Albany's son and successor Murdach Stewart. In consideration of this service, Duke Murdach gave his cousin half of the profits of the office of Justiciar of the north, and half of the rents of Badenoch, Urquhart, and Strathavon—an office and lands formerly possessed by the Wolf of Badenoch, the Earl's father.

The Earl of Mar had no issue by either of his wives, and he had only a liferent of the Earldom, but by this agreement he was to infeft his natural son Sir Thomas Stewart, in the Earldom, with remainder to the Duke of Albany and his heirs. Murdach agreed to confirm the deed, and to do his best to get the King to ratify it, and he further undertook to prevent, as far as he could, the marriage which his son Sir Walter Stewart of Lennox then contemplated with Janet Erskine, daughter of Sir Robert Erskine the legal heir to the Earldom of Mar in virtue of descent from Sir John Menteith and his wife Elene de Mar. There is reason to believe that Murdach failed in this last part of the bargain, as Sir Walter Stewart certainly obtained a Papal dispensation for his contemplated marriage in 1421, though there is no absolute proof that the union was actually consummated.

In 1424, King James returned to Scotland, and in the following year, Murdach Duke of Albany, and his sons Sir

Walter and Sir Alexander Stewart, were tried and executed—the Earl of Mar and his sons Sir Thomas Stewart and Sir John Stewart being required to act on the jury which tried them.

In 1426 King James confirmed Murdach's Charter in regard to the Earldom of Mar, substituting the Crown in the remainder, in place of Albany as in the original deed, a condition which in 1435 brought the Earldom to the Crown, to the injury of the legal heir, Robert Lord Erskine.

In 1431 the Earl of Mar and his cousin Alan Stewart Earl of Caithness (son of Walter, Earl of Athole) led the Royal army against Donald Balloch and a great Highland army and fleet at the Battle of Inverlochy. In that fatal field the young Earl of Caithness and sixteen of his relatives and personal retainers were slain. Many other barons also perished, and the Earl of Mar only succeeded in extricating the shattered remnants of his little army with great difficulty.

This is the last important appearance of this celebrated warrior. He died in 1434, and the following year—his son Thomas being then also dead—his Earldom reverted to the Crown.

The other son of King Robert II., to whom reference may here most conveniently be made, is David Stewart, the King's eldest son by his second marriage.

He seems, like his brother King Robert III., and unlike his other brothers, to have been a quiet and peaceable man, and makes little figure in history. On his father's accession to the throne he received a Charter of the Castle and Barony of Urquhart (19th June 1371). On 21st March 1374-75 he obtained the Castle of Braco and lands in Caithness. On 14th February 1380-81 he was created Earl of Strathearn, with Palatinate power, with remainder to his heirs male. In 1381-82 he had a safe-conduct to travel into England with forty horse. In the grant of lands he is spoken of by the King as "our most "beloved son." He died some time before 1389, leaving by his wife (whose name is unknown) an only daughter, the Lady Euphemia Stewart, who married Sir Patrick Graham (son of Sir Patrick Graham of Dundaff and Kincardine by his second wife Egidia Stewart of Railstoun), by whom the title of Earl of Strathearn was assumed in her supposed right. Sir Patrick Graham was killed in 1413 by Sir John Drummond, leaving an only child, Malise, likewise known as Earl of Strathearn. In his youth, Malise was sent into England as a hostage for the ransom of King James I., and there he seems to have fallen in love with Ann, daughter of Henry, Earl of Oxford. Returning to Scotland he found himself deprived of the Earldom of Strathearn on the ground that it was a male fief, and therefore not transmittable through females, it being part of King James' policy thus to weaken the power of the great lords, especially those who had come to the possession of their lands during his own captivity. Whether justifiable in strict law or not, the step was an impolitic one, and resulted in the King's murder in February 1437-38, for though, in exchange for the Earldom of Strathearn, which had been obtained by the crafty Earl of Athole, the King conferred on his young cousin and hostage, the Earldom of Menteith, this being an inferior honour, the transaction gave great offence to the Earl's uncle Sir Robert Graham. The incensed Graham renounced his allegiance, and forthwith proceeded to plot, along with other lords, for the murder of the King. The result is well known, and need not be retold here. It is sufficient to say that the party most concerned, Earl Malise himself, seems to have had no share in the treason, as he lived till 1492. By his wife Ann, daughter of the Earl of Oxford, he had three sons. From the eldest descended the Grahams, Earls of Menteith and Airth, and from the second, known for his valour as "Sir John with the bright "sword," descended the Viscount Preston who was attainted and forfeited for his loyalty to King James VII.

King Robert the Second seems to have been the first of the Scottish Kings to adopt a royal device.

The device and motto selected, though, considered separately, seemingly contradictory, are yet, in conjunction, not only in the finest harmony, but afford an interesting revelation of the inner nature and reverent and poetic instincts of the first of the Royal line of Stewart. A coronet decorated with rows of glittering stars, in combination with a terrestrial globe, might, by themselves, be ascribed to a heart consumed by vanity and pride, but the accompanying motto—

"Vanitas Vanitatum et omnia Vanitas"

indicates the good King's appreciation of the vanity of worldly grandeur, and the true significance which the device he had chosen conveyed to his own mind and was intended to convey to others.

In person, King Robert the Second was tall and majestic, and all the old historians unite in praising his exceptional stature and beauty of person. The qualities of his mind were equally attractive, and his unaffected humility and affability— rendering him easy of access to the meanest of his subjects— so endeared him to his people that what the Royal dignity might lose in the attributes of awe or pomp was more than gained in popular love and veneration.

In considering his character, the age in which he lived and its habits and customs must not be overlooked, nor can the standards and ideas of the present day in fairness be applied to him. If, according to the *outward* code of modern morality, King Robert's private life was not all it might or should have been, it ought not to be forgotten that in his day illegitimacy carried neither to parent nor offspring, the stigma and disgrace which it does in our time. On the contrary, the children born out of wedlock very commonly, as in the present instance, shared to the full with their more fortunate brothers, not only the affection and care of the parent, but his name, and, to some extent, his property. And in this view of the matter who shall say that the present age is after all so great an improvement on the old, since the stricter code of modern manners, by rendering it more imperative than of yore at whatever cost to cloak and hide the wounds of virtue from the world's censorious eye, has also unquestionably led to other sins, even against common humanity, at least as great as, if not worse than, those of an age at which, from out our robes of superior righteousness and vaunted greater purity, we are now apt to point the finger of scorn.

Apart however from this aspect, the character of King Robert is one which must command the admiration and respect, not only of those of kindred race and lineage, but of all who hold patriotism, and its allied virtues of courage, loyalty, and endurance, in honour.

Left an orphan almost in infancy, he was, when little more than a boy, forced out on the sea of life to battle with the waves and tempests of national enmities and ambitions, and the currents and quicksands of jealousy, envy, and rivalry, among his peers. He was scarcely seventeen when he drew his sword to oppose the invader and assert the freedom of his country, and the sword thus early unsheathed, was practically never laid aside from the same righteous quarrel throughout the whole course of his long life. Outlawed by the usurper Baliol, stripped of his high honours and vast estates, and driven to seek safety in concealment in a distant island, his courage never faltered, his patriotism and loyalty never wavered. By his own valour and address he recovered his inheritance from the enemy, and inspiring others by the brilliance of his exploits and example, with their help he swept the English forces out of Scotland, and restored his country's lost independence. Unswerving in his loyalty to his absent and subsequently captive uncle King David, he sought no personal advantage or gain from his labours in the common weal, and with memorable self-sacrifice and a fidelity ill repaid, he offered himself, his sons, and other relatives, as hostages for the freedom of his captive sovereign. Entrusted by his countrymen, long before maturity, with the rule and government of his native land and a fierce and high-spirited people, he found his country torn by faction, and its independence constantly threatened and attacked by the ambitions and encroachments of a vastly wealthier and more powerful neighbour. Yet even in the midst of a continual struggle against an enemy on his borders, he succeeded in maintaining some appearance of law and order, and that too in an age when the strong hand had hitherto been too much accustomed to make might right, and to subordinate justice to personal aims and ambitions.

The government of such a country as Scotland in his time was no light or easy task; and the obstacles and difficulties were greater than probably in any other European country. Different origin, language, and customs divided the North from the South, and the inhabitants of the Highlands, strangers to agriculture or industry, preyed on their lowland countrymen. David the Second obtained an appearance of peace and tranquillity, by inciting the chieftains to mutual destruction, under promise of gift of the lands of the vanquished to his conqueror. But such a policy of cruelty, abhorrent to the gentler nature of the Stewarts, was abandoned by King Robert, who entrusted the care of the Highlands to his heir, John, Earl of Carrick—afterwards " Robert III."

The administration of the law even in the lowlands was obstructed and made difficult by the conditions of feudal tenure, and by the power attained by the nobles during the long wars with England following on the death of Alexander III. The Bruses and the Stewarts had, within the course of less than

100 years from that event, themselves passed from the ranks of the nobility, to the Crown. Their reign was therefore at first unattended by the weight and influence of a long regal ancestry, or, as in England, by the awe of a foreign power; while they had to secure the loyalty of their former peers and equals, by lavish rewards which in many cases only served to weaken the Crown which they were intended to strengthen.

Nor must it be forgotten that in that age the King had only nominal command of the army—the military forces being simply the individual retainers of the great lords and nobles, who were frequently disaffected to, if not in actual rebellion against, the law, and sometimes even against the Crown itself. This fact alone goes far to explain the difficulty experienced by King Robert in establishing order, while his task was further aggravated by the fact that the Sovereign, in the great majority of cases, did not possess even the nomination, much less the choice, of his officers of justice. These offices were almost always enjoyed by hereditary right, and experience had shown that any attempt to interfere with such rights—as in the case of Sir Alexander Ramsay and the Black Knight of Liddisdale, in the reign of David II.— was itself calculated to lead to crime and cruelty of the most fearful description. The barons usually had the power of life and death—the right of pit and gallows—in their own terri- tories, and the execution of the law, so far as those territories were concerned, was in great measure dependent on the satisfaction or dissatisfaction of the baron, with the Crown or his neighbours, for the time.

The vast hereditary possessions of the Stewarts might at first sight have seemed such as to furnish a military strength sufficient to overawe any individual subject however powerful. But their lands unfortunately were scattered throughout nearly every county south of Forth and Clyde, and thus the military strength of the Stewarts, in emergency lacked the cohesion which other great families, and notably the rival house of Douglas, enjoyed from the compactness and solidity of their territorial possessions. Had the lands of the Douglasses been as detached and isolated as those of the Stewarts, it is safe to say that family would never have been so formidable to the Crown as it ultimately became.

That King Robert, in spite of so many and so serious difficulties and disadvantages, yet succeeded in introducing and establishing considerable improvements in the internal government of his country, historians are generally agreed. Particularly were his efforts directed towards making property more secure, and life more sacred, from violence than they had been, and though his wise and judicious policy and pacific desires were all too frequently frustrated by his unruly barons, to whom the pomp and panoply of war were ever more congenial and attractive than all the benefits and blessings of peace, yet to him must be given the credit of striving to do his country solid service rather than to astonish it by deeds or

X

actions, which, however brilliant, would yet have conferred no lasting benefit or gain on his people.

His character as a Sovereign and as a man has been impartially summed up by the historian Pinkerton, whose words seem no unfitting epitaph with which to say farewell to the first of the Royal House of Stewart :—

" In the more difficult and more truly glorious arts of " peace, he is entitled to considerable praise. The terrors of " justice he knew how to deal impartially to the guilty, while " he opened every gate of protection to the innocent. His " actions proceeded in a solid and rational tenor, and his " promise was the exact standard of his performance. Internal " discords his equity appeased; and though his own age and " the infirmity of the apparent heir rendered his reign feeble, " yet his wisdom prevented it from being unfortunate.

" In a word, he is little known to history, because he was " a good King and a good man."

VANITAS VANITATUM ET OMNIA VANITAS.

INDEX.

GEO. STEWART & CO.,
PRINTERS,
92 GEORGE STREET, EDINBURGH.

1204867

Made in the USA

RESOURCES

American Association of Diabetes Educators
http://www.aadenet.org
(800) 338-3633

American Diabetes Association
http://www.diabetes.org
(800) 232-3472

American Dietetic Association
http://www.eatright.org
(800) 877-1600

Children with Diabetes
http://www.childrenwithdiabetes.com

Diabetes Exercise & Sports Association
http://www.diabetes-exercise.org
(800) 898-4322

International Diabetes Center
http://www.idcpublishing.com
(888) 637-2675

Joslin Diabetes Center
http://www.joslin.org
(612) 732-2400

Juvenile Diabetes Research Foundation International
http://www.jdrf.org
(800) 533-2873

National Diabetes Information Clearinghouse
http://diabetes.niddk.nih.gov
(800) 860-8747

Fasting blood glucose: a glucose level taken after at least 8 hours without food or other caloric intake.

Gestational diabetes: diabetes that develops or is first discovered in women during pregnancy.

Glucose: the medical term for sugar in the blood.

Insulin: a hormone made in the pancreas that allows glucose to enter cells, where it is used for energy.

Insulin pump: a small computer that releases insulin continuously to regulate blood glucose levels.

Insulin resistance: the body does not respond to or use insulin efficiently, which often results in high glucose levels.

Islets of Langerhans: clusters or groups of beta cells within the pancreas that make insulin. (Named after Paul Langerhans, who described them in 1869.)

Pancreas: the insulin-producing gland located behind the stomach.

Pre-diabetes: slightly elevated blood glucose levels (between 100-125 fasting, or 140-200 with food), which are not quite high enough for a diabetes diagnosis.

Sliding scale insulin: changing the insulin dose based on blood glucose values.

Type 1 diabetes: the body makes little or no insulin. (Formerly called juvenile-onset, Type I, or insulin-dependent diabetes.)

Type 2 diabetes: the body doesn't make enough insulin, or the insulin doesn't work like it should. (Formerly called adult-onset, Type II, or non-insulin-dependent diabetes.)

DEFINITIONS

A1C: a blood test that measures a 3-month blood glucose average, given in a percentage that shows overall diabetes control. (Also called HbA1C or hemoglobin A1C.) Experts recommend an A1C of less than 7%, which compares to a 150 blood glucose average.

Blood glucose monitor: a device that detects glucose levels within a small drop of blood placed on a test strip inside the monitor.

Blood sugar: layperson's term for blood glucose.

Carbohydrates: an energy-rich food nutrient. Found in all fruits, vegetables, grains, beans, milk, and yogurt, carbohydrates (also called carbs, starch, or sugar) break down easily into glucose for energy.

Cells: the smallest component of the body, visible only through a microscope.

Diabetes: a lifelong condition that interferes with the body's ability to get energy from food, resulting in high levels of blood glucose. For a diagnosis of diabetes, blood glucose values must be more than or equal to 126 fasting overnight, or above 200 any time of the day with symptoms, no matter what was eaten.

Diabetes care team: a group of medical professionals who help people live with diabetes. Examples include: primary care physician, endocrinologist, certified diabetes educator, registered nurse, registered dietitian, medical social worker, podiatrist, and ophthalmologist.

Diabetes symptoms: classic symptoms include profound thirst, hunger, increased urination, or unexplained weight loss; other common symptoms include fatigue, blurry vision, numbness or tingling in the feet.